PROPERTY
LIBRARY
Rose City Park Presbyterian Church
Sandy Boulevard at N. E. 44th Ave.
PORTLAND. OREGON

C0-DAM-801

AROUND
PORTLAND
WITH
KIDS

JUDI SIEWERT KATHRYN WEIT

Edited by Diane Sichel
Graphics by Carolyn Davidson
Photographs by Judi Siewert

Copyright © by Judi Siewert and Kathryn Weit
All Rights Reserved
Printed in the United States
Published by Discovery Press
P.O. Box 12241
Portland, Or. 97212
ISBN: 0-961426-0-1

DEDICATED TO OUR PARENTS

Louise and Evans Davis

and

Ken and Polly Reuhl

ACKNOWLEDGEMENTS

Special thanks to our supportive husbands, Bob and Ramsay, and for our understanding kids, Alisha, Justin and Kary Siewert and Colin and Jessica Weit.

And a special thanks to those people whose contributions have helped to make this book possible.

Catherine Gleason, Metro Arts Commision

Barbara Fritzler, Vancouver

The helpful people at City Planning, Metro Solid Waste, and Portland Water Bureau.

Kathryn's father, Ken, for hours of typing.

Judi's mother, Louise, for extended grandparenting and proofing.

2407

CONTENTS

INTRODUCTION

When people ask what to do with children, suggestions tend to be the old favorites like the Zoo and OMSI. These attractions, of course, are not to be missed, but there is more, much more in the Portland metropolitan area. In **Around Portland With Kids** we give you ideas on what to do and where to go. Ideas we have explored, researched and sampled firsthand. Hopefully, our book will stimulate your curiosity, as it did ours, to discover Portland and the metropolitan area, whether it's with a guide or on an adventure of your own.

The excursions and activities are designed for children and adults to do together. This is not only for safety, but also to give adults and children an opportunity to enjoy and share an adventure together. To help make your experiences more enjoyable, we've included a list of suggestions.

• Have a day pack, just for explorations, always ready and waiting. This will eliminate last minute searches and the "we forgot's" that can frustrate both children and adults. Items to pack:

   — Several plastic bags for carrying first-aid supplies (band-aids and cotton balls sprayed with antiseptic); extra bags for treasures, tissues and trash.

   — A map of the city to use for directions and to mark with colored stickers the places you have visited.

   — Binoculars for finding wildlife, or searching out landmarks from viewpoints.

- Call ahead for current information on hours, costs, and any special requirements for handicap access. We have tried to be accurate, but changes occur. Symbols used in this book:

- To preserve memories, don't forget to bring a camera (with film) and flash when appropriate.
- Make a habit of bringing along small notebooks and pencils for keeping a journal of discoveries.
- Return to sites to observe the changes of time and season.
- Always let someone know where you are going and when you expect to return.
- Many of the places in this book are on or near private property. Please be considerate, stay on trails and be responsible for your own litter.

We welcome any comments, suggestions or additions you might wish to make. Write us at Discovery Press, P.O. Box 12241, Portland, Or. 97212.

WALKS

Only minutes away from downtown Portland you can take a sidewalk stroll along the river or a deep woods hike. There are walks and hikes for little tots and more daring ones for older children. You can choose hikes with a variety of lengths and difficulty, from quiet to noisy, from mossy carpets to platforms in space.

Enjoy Portland outdoors, rain or shine!

Bridge Walk
Circle tour across Hawthorne Bridge, Eastside Esplanade. Morrison Bridge and Tom McCall Waterfront Park.

Portland is a city of many bridges, but we seldom take time to enjoy them by foot. This tour offers you a closeup look at two of Portland's bridges, plus unique views of the city and waterfront. When you walk the bridges look up and down the river to see the different types and uses of the bridges crossing the Willamette River. Notice the styles of opening and closing. Portland has drawbridges , and other that swivel and lift.

Note: Because of the secluded areas included in this outing, we strongly recommend that the walk be done in a small group. We also suggest that you avoid peak traffic hours when bridge traffic is fast and furious. There is no handicap access on some sections of this hike. Despite the drawbacks, this is an adventure walk that should not be missed.

Directions: Park on west side near the Hawthorne Bridge. Take the stairs on north side of bridge, staying on the north sidewalk. Crossing the bridge, note the Eastside Esplanade and fire station directly north. This is where you're heading.

At east end of the bridge, take stairs going down to vacant parking lots. Walk through lots to the fire station with Esplanade entrance directly north at Third and Main. Head north to winding ramp leading to Morrison Bridge. Walk up ramp and across the bridge using the south sidewalk. At the end of the bridge head down the ramp at Front Avenue. Take stairs under street to Tom McCall Waterfront Park and continue along seawall south back to the Hawthorne Bridge.

Eastside Esplanade
Runs along the eastside of the Willamette River from the Hawthorne Bridge to the Burnside Bridge

The Eastside Esplanade offers a marvelous view of the downtown skyline and Portland's bridges that we usually see only fleetingly as we rush by in speeding cars. The walk is particularly pleasant in the late Spring when azaleas planted along the Esplanade are in full bloom.
Note: Because of the secluded locations of the Esplanade, we strongly recommend that this walk only be done with family or friends. Although the walkway is wide, there are steep drops to the water in places. The freeway is immediately to the right on the other side of a cyclone fence.

Directions: Take Water Street, turn toward river onto SE Main. Go to the end of the street and park. Fire station is on the left, entrance to the Esplanade is to the right.

Macleay Park-Balch Canyon
Entrance to Lower Macleay Trail at NW 30th and Upshur.

The Balch Canyon/Lower Macleay trail is rated tops for beginning hikers. The trail winds through deep forest along rushing Balch stream. There are wooden bridges to cross, waterfalls, and mossy pools. Hike here year round, but because there are so many deciduous trees it is particularly beautiful in the autumn. For a little more challenging hike, continue on until the trail connects with the Wildwood Trail into Macleay Park on NW Cornell Road. After 1.25 miles on this section of the trail you will see the moss-covered stone house, a favorite place for children to climb in and around. A great place to tell a fairy tale.

Directions: Entrance to Lower Macleay Trail at NW 30 and Upshur.

**Portland Audubon Society
5151 N Cornell Road
Portland, 292-6855
Hours: Daily, 10 to 5**

Start your hike with a stop at Audubon House. Here you will find information about trails, wildlife, Audubon activities, and you can pick up crushed corn to feed the ducks in the pond below. Also at Audubon House is an extensive bookstore focusing on the Northwest outdoors. There are several trails, about .6 of a mile each, which wind through woods and meadows.

The Audubon Society sponsors programs and many educational activities for children and adults. Call for information.

Note: Good for beginning hikers and an excellent place to bring binoculars for bird watching.

Directions: Take NW Lovejoy west to Cornell Road.

**Oaks Bottom Wildlife Refuge
Below Sellwood Park at SE Seventh and Miller**

Oaks Bottom Wildlife Refuge is 110 acres of river bottom habitat on the east side of the Willamette River. It is one of the choice wildlife habitats in the Portland city limits and a favorite for bird watchers. We saw several blue heron, pheasants, and ducks in one short morning stroll. This is a good walk for people of almost any age.

Note: Great for bird watching and small wildlife, so be sure to bring binoculars.

Directions: Begin hike at northwest end of Sellwood Park near parking lot. A marked trail meanders downhill through the woods. At the base of the hill, bear right into the wildlife refuge.

Leif Erikson Road

Leif Erikson Road was once the main road through Forest Park. Now closed to vehicular traffic, it is a favorite of walkers and joggers year round. The temperature always seems to be at least 10 degrees cooler here than in the city. If you have the time and inclination, you can hike over 7 miles on Leif Erikson Road. The roadway intersects the ubiquitous Wildwood Trail (the main Hoyt Arboretum/Forest Park Hiking Trails) in many places and it is possible to take walks deeper into Forest Park. If you want something much shorter, there are also rewards. Just beyond the 1/4 mile marker is a turnout with a spectacular view of Mount Hood, Mount St. Helens, the Fremont Bridge, Port of Portland, and Portland's east side.

Note: Trail is a dirt/gravel road with a gradual incline. Good for beginning as well as experienced hikers. Roadway has distance markers.
Directions: Follow NW Thurman to the very end where it becomes a dirt road. Park the car along roadside when you come to the gate. Hike begins here.

Hoyt Arboretum
**4000 SW Fairview Blvd.
Portland, 228-8732**

The 200-plus acre Hoyt Arboretum contains a collection of more than 650 species of trees and shrubs from all over the world and has the largest grouping of conifers in the world. This lush park, five minutes from city center, has more than 10 miles of trails and meadows, including a paved trail with wheelchair access. A great spot to hike and picnic.

A sampling of the trails are:

• Redwood Trail: Begins by shelter, circles and ends by shelter. Mainly conifers, this trail is usually shady on a hot day and also offers more protection on rainy days. Trail is approximately 1 mile. Wheelchairs and strollers possible.

• Oak Trail: Begins and ends by Tree House. Primarily deciduous trees, this is a good place to see flowering trees in the spring.

• Bristlecone Pine: Paved level trail, designed for handicapped access. To get to trail, drive past shelter and Tree House on SW Fairview. Make a left on SW Fischer Lane. Parking lot on left is the start of the trail. Approximately 1/4 mile.

These three trails have self-guided tour books that can be obtained for a small fee at the Tree House. Arboretum staff also provide guided tours for children. Call for information. **Note:** Some of the trails get muddy after a few days of rain.

Directions: Follow directions from Washington Park Zoo. When you come to Fairview, turn right. Park at shelter. The Tree House, the visitors center offering trail guides and information, is across the street.

Marquam Trail
Portland, 228-8732
Council Crest Park to SW Sam Jackson Parkway

The Marquam Trail winds down through a deep wooded canyon and along a forest stream for part of the way. The total hike from Council Crest to the Marquam shelter is about 2 miles. Starting the trail at Council Crest can be somewhat difficult because people seem to remove the sign posts. Look directly below the Council Crest lookout and face east. You will see a large grassy area with a big clump of deciduous trees. Begin walking along the edge of the hill here and you will find paths leading into the woods which link to the Marquam Trail. Look for the sign in the woods that marks the trail.

To prevent getting sidetracked, stay on the most heavily traveled trail. At several points you will see other trails, but these lead to private residences. Where the trail splits, take a left, going downhill. Continue down this trail to the Marquam Hill shelter on Sam Jackson Parkway. From here The Carnival Restaurant, a traditional favorite of Portland families, is just a short walk to the left, down Sam Jackson Parkway.

The trail is for the average to good hiker, and crosses roadways at several points. The section of the hike between Greenway and Fairmont is short and level, an excellent trail for very young hikers, and can be taken as a separate walk.

Guided tours are offered spring and fall. Call Hoyt Arboretum and specify the Marquam Trail.

Note: Trail can be muddy in places.

Directions: Because this trail is largely downhill, this is a good place to use the two-car shuttle system if possible. Park one car at the base of the trail at the Marquam Trail shelter and then drive to begin trail at Council Crest Park.

Himes Park to Willamette Park
SW Terwilliger & Savin Road
Portland

A deep-woods walk that is wonderful on hot summer days. At the top, Himes Park is a small, flat, deeply shaded area with picnic tables. The trail winds down the canyon and continues under Barbur Blvd. and the freeway. Approximately 1 1/2 miles more through residental neighborhoods you will reach Willamette Park.

Note: Trail can be muddy and quite steep in parts. Not recommended for beginning hikers.

Directions: To get to Himes Park take Terwilliger north. Make a left on Nebraska and park by Himes Park. If you choose to hike all the way to Willamette Park, it would be best to use a two-car shuttle.

Forest Park—Wildwood Trail

Forest Park is 4,700 acres, 8 miles long and 1 1/2 miles wide, on the northwest hills of Portland. It contains more than 50 miles of trails. The park extends from Burnside Steet on the south, to Newberry Road on the north; from St. Helens Road on the east to Skyline on the west. There are numerous points of access.

Maps of Forest Park are available at many locations including the Portland Visitors Center at 26 SW Salmon, Audubon House and Hoyt Arboretum. The map contains a trail log (distances) from point to point, side trail lengths, and a profile of the Wildwood Trail. This map also shows areas of direct auto access.

Here are two sections of the Wildwood Trail particularly good for children:

• **Japanese Garden:** Walk or ride truck from the entrance of the Japanese Garden on SW Knight up hill to garden. Trail is outside garden and follows ledge above.It is possible to look down into parts of the garden.

• **Pittock Mansion:** 3229 NW Pittock Dr. See signs for Pittock Mansion on W Burnside. Trail begins at Pittock Mansion, in the northwest corner of parking lot. Trail goes down wooded hillside and can be quite steep in places.

Lewis & Clark College
615 SW Palatine Hill Road
Portland, 244-6161

The Frank (Meier & Frank) estate is the heart of the Lewis & Clark campus.

This is a walk around the grounds of the old estate with some possible side trips into the woods nearby. A great outing for families with young children. Walk behind the old estate house. The grounds are in large tiers. There are two stone gazebos, small ponds with fountains, and there is a reflecting pool that is great for sailing toy boats. Below the reflecting pool is a swimming pool which is open to the public. Near the pool are two beautiful grape arbors with picnic tables. A wonderful place to cool off on a hot day. Further down the hillside is a large and well maintained rose garden.

Note: Probably best to do this outing when the college is not in session or on weekends, as parking can sometimes be a problem.

Directions: I-5 to Terwilliger Exit. Turn left off Terwilliger to Palatine Hill Road, enter Lewis & Clark College through main gates to center of campus, near library. May have to park by main gate. Begin walk behind old estate house to right of library.

Crystal Springs Creek
Reed College Campus
SE 28th, one block north of Woodstock

This walk explores the headwaters of Crystal Springs Creek. From SE 28th, turn into Reed College and park down by the theater. Walk up the roadway toward the Reed College swimming pool and you will see Reed Lake, usually full of hungry ducks. Follow the trail around the pond. (Muddy when wet.) When you come to the bridge you can either go across, or walk a little further into the marsh area. The marsh is the origin of Crystal Springs Creek. There are lots of birds and frogs.

To continue the walk, backtrack and cross the bridge, following the trail the rest of the way around the pond. You will see where the stream leaves the pond and you can follow it a short distance past the swimming pool, through the field. Here the stream is only a few feet wide and rapidly moving.

Crystal Springs Creek continues, flowing through the Rhododendron Garden, Westmoreland Park, and Johnson Creek Park. (see **PARKS**)

Oregon City Promenade
Located in the upper part of historical Oregon City

The Promenade runs along a windy bluff overlooking the Willamette River in Oregon City, once capital of Oregon Territory. Walking south from the elevator you will have a bird's eye view of Publisher's Paper. The Willamette Falls are spectacular from here and you get a sense of the awe original settlers must have felt. Heading north, the Promenade goes a short distance to stairs that will take you under Singer Hill

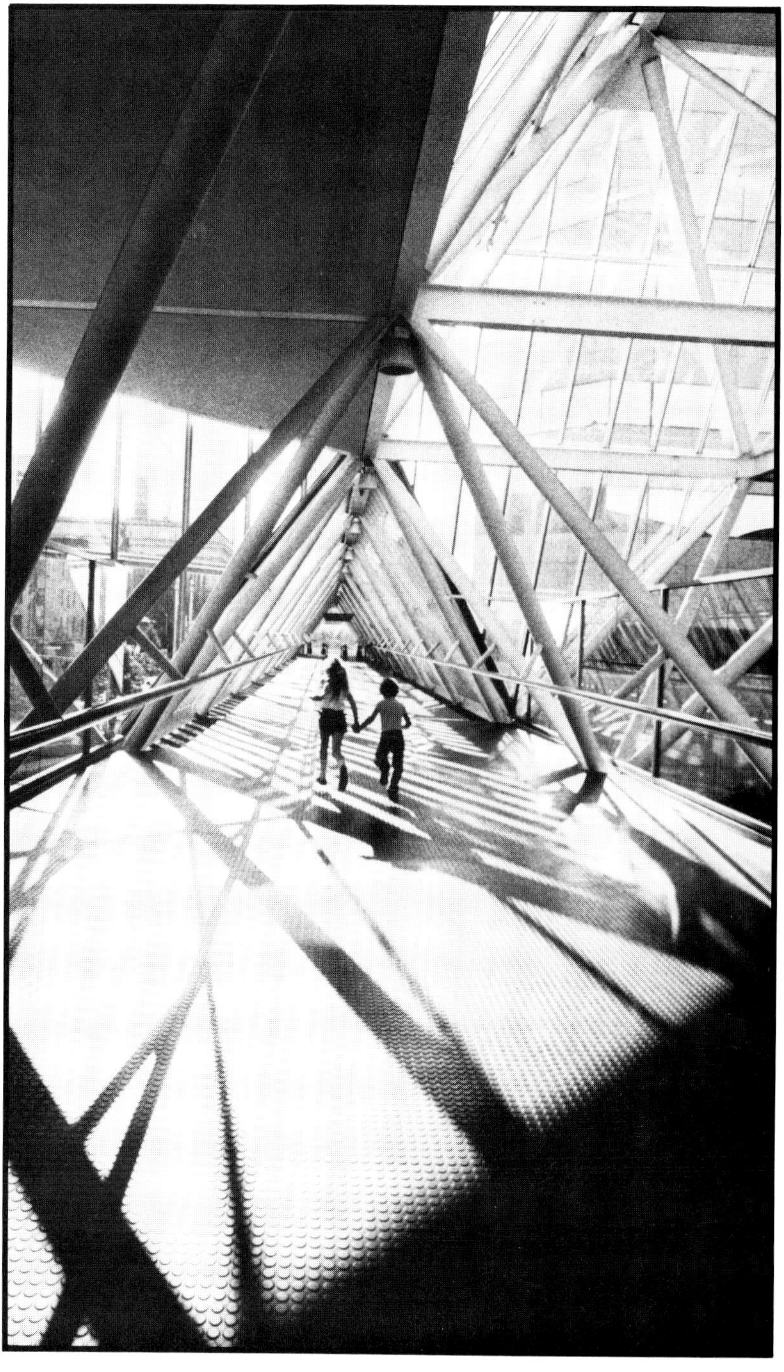

Street, through a tunnel to the McLoughlin House Museum and other historic houses. Continue down the stairs alongside cascading pools of water, known as Singer Falls, to the foot of the bluff.

Note: Elevator is free. Good place for binoculars. Good for strollers and wheelchairs.

Directions: Park your car near the Oregon City Municipal Elevator (Corner of Seventh and Railroad Avenue). Take elevator up to Promenade.

Jantzen Beach

A short, paved walkway overlooking the Columbia River, offering great views of houseboats, river traffic, swans and ducks. It's in the flight path of Portland's International Airport, so the airplanes fly low overhead.

Note: This is a pleasant, easy walk for beginning hikers.

Directions: Jantzen Beach exit off I-5. Park near Jantzen Beach bowling lanes at the south end of Jantzen Beach Shopping Mall. Walk toward water and turn right. The walk begins about 1/2 block from Jantzen Beach lanes, opposite Building A. Past ramp 6, the walkway makes a half circle, ending behind the Toys R' Us store.

Willamette Center Space Walk
121 SW Salmon St.
Portland, 226-5757
Hours: Avoid business hours. Weekends and evenings best.

Imagine being on a space station. Strolling along the glass enclosed skywalks is a great way to project yourself into the future. The skywalks span the streets and offer interesting views of the river. Traffic noise is practically nil so bring a lunch and picnic at the colorful tables under glass. Great for rainy days.

Note: The escalators are closed on weekends so use the stairs on Second and Salmon. There is an elevator inside the building just behind the carousel, on First, next to Edison's Restaurant.

Tryon Creek State Park (see PARKS)

EXCURSIONS

These adventures are designed for adults to share with children. We hope these experiences will help your children to better understand and enjoy the community, city, and, perhaps, the world they live in. The people involved with these activities are open to visits. We ask, however, that even though some of these excursions are designed to be less formal and even spontaneous, that you be sensitive to the interests, age and size of your group. Please be aware of busy days and hours of the place you visit and enter and leave with little disturbance.

It is our hope that this section of the book will inspire you to discover your own adventures in our city.

AIRPORTS

AAR—Western Skyways
Troutdale, 665-1181
Troutdale Airport—East I-84. Take Troutdale Airport Exit—17. Monday-Friday, 8-5. Group tours available with two week notice.

This is a small airport and a part of the Port of Portland Airport system. Visit the flight office, the propeller shop, and see the repairing and washing of planes. With a group, it is possible to arrange a discount on an airplane ride.

Port of Portland International Airport

This is Portland's largest airport serving both domestic and international flights. You will see all types of aircraft—large and small. For a formal tour call 231-5000.

Aurora Airport
Take I-5 south to Aurora-Canby exit, and go east to Airport Road.

You'll see close-up the daily activities of a small airport. There are helicopters and small aircraft landing and taking off. You'll see the refueling, repairing and washing of planes. Check in at the flight office before you wander around.

Columbia Helicopter
Aurora-Canby Airport, 657-1111
Ardt Road, north end of airport.

See helicopters being repaired. This is one of the few places in the country that repairs helicopters. Best to go during the winter months when the helicopters are in for their yearly check-ups.

Aircraft At Your Call
Hillsboro Airport, 640-8294

A variety of aircraft from small planes to corporate jets. Group tours available. For a visit to the tower, call 648-5880. Tours for children over age 12. It is possible, however, to visit the tower with a younger child, and in very small groups, during slow periods. Must call ahead.

Hillsboro Helicopter
Hillsboro Airport, 1040 NE 25, 648-2831

Another airport operated by the Port of Portland. Home of the Skyview Traffic Watch, which you hear on the radio monitoring traffic flow throughout the day. A good place to view small airport operations. Helicopter rides are available for children two years and older. Saturday is the best day to visit.

Portland Air Base
6801 NE Cornfoot Rd., 288-5611
South end of Portland International Airport—signs off Lombard Blvd. Enter at Jernstedt Gate. Informal tours mid-morning during weekdays.

This base houses the Army National Guard, Air Force Reserve, and the Air National Guard. These military organizations serve our state in air/search and rescue—from assisting in finding lost mountain climbers to assisting in local disasters. When Mount St. Helens blew, they rescued 65 people.

See the flight line with the F4C Phantom jets, the mobile communications systems, and visit the classroom and squadron headquarters. There are also helicopters, trucks and jeeps.

INDUSTRIAL TOURS BY CAR

A great look at some of Portland's busiest industrial areas. You'll see the heavy metal and shipping industries and some gigantic sandpiles.

Ross Island Area
Off Harbor Way take Sheridan Street to Moody. To make a circle take Gibbs, off Moody, to Bond. Turn right at Abernathy, up to Moody, and connect back up to Harbor Way.

See some of the city's largest sandpiles and the front and side yards of Zidells salvage company. Watch out for large dump trucks rushing back and forth to load and deliver sand throughout the city.

Giles Lake Area
Off US Highway 30, take 29th north to Yeon. Head northeast to Kittridge Avenue. Turn east to Front Street. Head south, making a circle out onto Nicolai Street, to Highway 30.

This area was once a large lake and included a large pavilion, the center of activity during the Lewis & Clark Exposition in 1905. Drive by heavy metal factories, along the railyards and close to the port action at Terminal No. 2. Quite a different environment from the early 1900's.

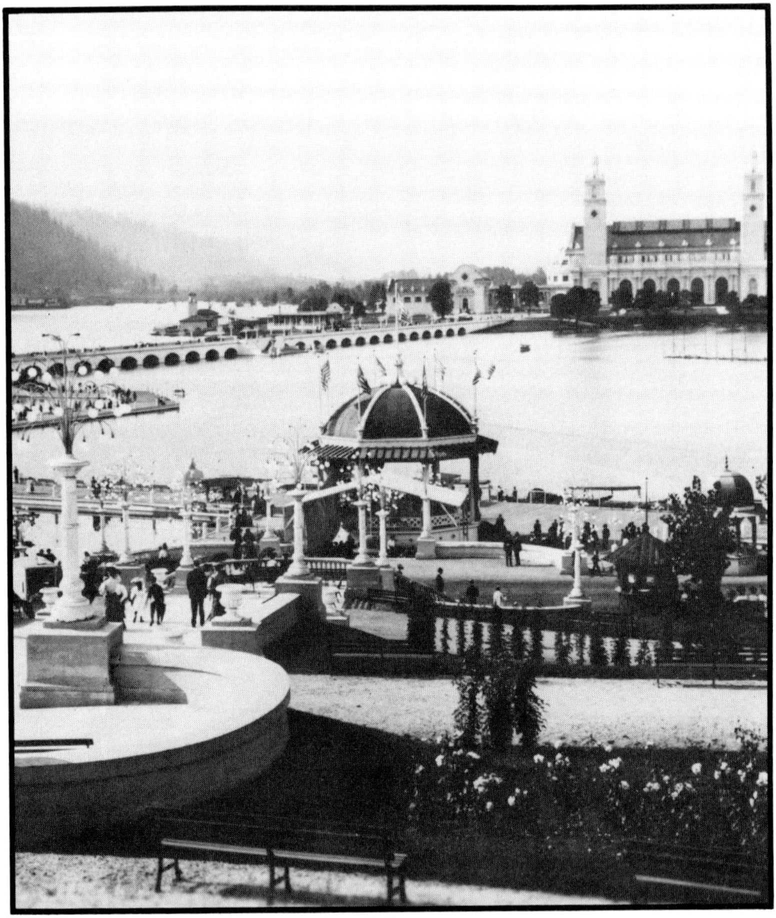

MUNICIPAL TOURS

City Hall
1220 SW Fifth
Portland, 226-3161

This is the place to watch and listen to city council meetings. They take place on the second floor, every Wednesday, at 9:30 am, and again at 2 pm until adjournment. For council agenda, call 248-4086. Meetings are open to the public and sometimes offer quite a cast of characters and interesting subjects. If time permits, you may be able to visit the mayor's office; call ahead for a visit—248-4120.

Pioneer Court House and U.S. Post Office
Portland
Between Fifth and Sixth Avenue, and Morrison and Yamhill Streets.

When you enter on Sixth Avenue, you'll see two large caryatids on each side of the doorway. Just inside the US Post Office are many old photographs and drawings of early Portland. Here is housed the Federal Court of Appeals. The courtrooms are open to the public.

There is a cupola located on top of the building. (see **VIEWS**).

Justice Center
1120 SW Third Ave.
Portland

The Justice Center replaced the old Rocky Butte Jail. The building houses several operations, including the jail, central police headquarters, two Circuit Courts, and two District Courts. A prisoner can be booked, held, arraigned and serve a sentence, all in one building. Due to the open-courtyard concept in housing prisoners, tours of the jail are not available for people under 18 years of age. However, the jail lobby and courtrooms are open to the public.

For tours of the police precinct, call 796-3020.

Post Office

Visit your neighborhood post office. If you call ahead you'll get a tour behind the scenes. For information, see US Postal Service, in the phone book. Ask for station manager. Never call in December.

Portland Building
1150 SW Fifth
Portland, 226-3161

Here are located the offices of the county and city employees, representing the various bureaus that make our city and county tick. There is a viewing gallery on the second floor with changing exhibits. Also on the second floor are several meeting rooms where you may hear citizens with complaints or requests presenting their problems to the various bureaus. In Room C, there is a beautiful wooden replica of the downtown area, built to scale. A must see before or after a city tour.

Police Precincts
4735 E. Burnside (East), 248-5696
7214 N. Philadelphia (North), 248-5720

Ask for the crime prevention person at each precinct and they will gladly help with your visit.

See the officers' lockers, patrol cars, gauges, and equipment. You may see police procedures such as ticketing and bookings. Portland's own "Hill Street Blues".

Fire Station

Visit your neighborhood fire station first. For information, call 248-4375, and ask for the public education officer to learn the address and number of the fire station nearest you.

The largest fire station in Portland is located at 55 SW Ash. In addition to seeing the fire trucks and usual fire fighting equipment, firemen will demonstrate their pole-sliding abilities. Located within the station is the fire department museum. Here you will see Portland's early fire-fighting equipment, learn about the fire brigades of the past, and view museum pictures.

LIVE AUDIENCE TV

The Rambling Rod Show
KPTU, Channel 12
735 SW 20th Place
Portland, 222-9921

A special treat to take a birthday person, but need to make a reservation more than six months in advance.

AM/NW Show
KATU, Channel 2
2153 NE Sandy Blvd.
Portland, 231-4610

A local morning talk show program with national and local guests offering a wide variety of subjects. Each summer an entire week is devoted to just kids.

Two at Four
KATU, Channel 2
2153 NE Sandy Blvd.
Portland, 231-4250

Similar format as the morning show, but at 4 pm.

MISCELLANEOUS

Portland Opera Costume Shop
1301 NW Glisan
Portland, 224-6687

To visit, you must call ahead. The shop has more than 8,000 costumes from various Portland Opera productions. You can see the creation of a costume—from sketches to the finished product. We suggest that you visit five to six weeks prior to the opening of the opera, then return to see the finished costume and, of course, attend an opera to see how it all comes together. The shop will also visit schools to put on a demonstration, bringing their wigs, make-up and costumes. The demonstration involves choosing students from the audience and dressing them as characters from an opera.

Canby Forest Nursery (Industrial Forest Association)
1887 N Holly St.
Canby, 266-7825

There are 106 acres of seedlings, including noble and Douglas fir, ponderosa pine, Sitka spruce and hemlock. The seedlings are used for reforestation. You can see the nursery from the road, but if you'd like a guided tour, just call ahead. Tours include explanations of soil preparation, seeding and planting, weeding, cultivations, irrigation, root pruning and frost protection. Since seedlings grow for two or three years and in the same place, this would be a good place to return to observe change. It takes a long time to produce a forest!

Clackamas Fish Hatchery
Estacada, 630-7210
Call ahead if you bring a large group. Out of Estacada, take highway 224 and look for signs to McIver Park—located on the Clackamas River.

The fish hatchery is open from 7:30 to 4:30, seven days a week, year round. Summer and spring are the best times to see spring Chinook Salmon. After October, only the fingerlings (babies) are left. There are two large rearing ponds and other ponds for adult fish.

Sauvie Island
Located 13 miles north of Portland, off Highway 30.

This is an area with more than 12,000 acres of lakes, beaches, farmland and river bottom habitat. The island is a major winter resting area for a large number of waterfowl. More than 300,000 ducks, geese, swans, heron and cranes can be see here, and an occasional bald eagle. Sturgeon Lake is a great place for fishing. There are several farms with U-pick vegetables, fruit and berries.

A favorite is the Pumpkin Patch where you can see barns, farm animals, vegetable fields and a farm stand. Tours are available for groups: Call 621-3874 or 621-3316. During the Halloween season, it's a special place to find a pumpkin. See the "Spooky Pumpkin field" and share a cup of apple cider.

The Annual "Wintering in Festival" is held in the early fall at the Bybee-Howell Territorial Park. Also the site of the Children's Agricultural Museum — a step back in time to see what it was like growing up on a frontier farm. (see **MUSEUMS**).

Wilhelm Farms
6001 SW Meridian Way
Tualatin, 638-5387

There are barns with all types of farm animals. During the Halloween and Christmas seasons, you can enjoy hay rides and a ride in a surrey. During Christmas, a Nativity Pageant takes place in one of the barns.

Vegetables and fruit are available for picking and purchase from April through December.

Western Forestry Center
4033 SW Canyon Rd.
Portland, 228-1367
Hours: daily, 10-5 pm.

Multimedia exhibits explain the history of forests and the forestry industry in Oregon. There are interesting Tom Hardy sculptures, a talking tree and a model sawmill. An extensive collection of wood samples from all over the world cover almost an entire floor.

There are changing exhibits. Many, like the wooden toy and doll house shows, are of particular interest to children.

Children can climb into the 1909 Shay steam engine, a logging locomotive, located outside the Forestry Center. Call for specific information about the changing exhibits and classes.

Washington Park Zoo (**$**)
4001 SW Canyon Rd.
Portland, 226-7617 Zoo Recording, 226-1561 Switchboard.
Hours: Daily, summer 9:30-7; Daily, winter 9:30-4; Tuesday after 3 pm free.

The Washington Park Zoo continues to be a perennial favorite for children of all ages. The Zoo has a national reputation for its Asian Elephant herd. Jane Goodall, the famous zoologist, advised on the design of the extensive chimpanzee habitat. The Cascade Stream and Pond Exhibit gives you a peek into a beaver hut and you can get nose to nose with a penguin in the Penguin House.

The Zoo also offers classes and camps. Call the switchboard for more information. The Zoo Train (see **RIDES**) and the Ladybug Theater (see **ARTS**) are located at the Washington Park Zoo.

Storybook Rockery
Rt. 6, Box 796
Hillsboro
Hours: Open daily, 628-1575. Call ahead.

A path goes around the yard to the back where you'll find detailed houses, castles, and characters in their storybook settings. All of the buildings are done in stone with small signs in front of each. During the spring and summer, ground coverings are in bloom around the area giving the place an added charm.

Directions: Seven miles west of Beaverton on Farmington Rd. Look for the green house with white trim on the right and a big red barn on the left. If you come to River Road and Twin Oaks Tavern you've gone too far.

Lone Fir Cemetery
Between SE Morrison and Stark, and 20th and 26th Street. Portland, 248-3622 (Pioneer Cemeteries).
Hours: Mon.-Fri., 8 to 4.

A walk through Portland's oldest cemetery offers a view of both the good and the tragic of Portland history. You will find the famous and the infamous buried here, including the much photographed gravestone carved with the likeness of the pioneers James and Elizabeth Stephens. The large vault and chapel was built for the Macleay family. Asa Lovejoy, who lost in the the coin toss to name the city, is buried here; and sections near the Multnomah County building were originally a Chinese graveyard. At one time there were thousands of Chinese graves, but many have since been returned to China. There are over 23,000 graves at Lone Fir dating before 1900. The earliest is 1846. As many of the original markers were carved in wood and have disappeared with time, many graves are now unmarked. By 1928, the cemetery was so rundown that Multnomah County assumed control. The Pioneer Cemetery office, 2115 SE Morrison, has brochures of Lone Fir that include history and maps of the cemetery.

Visit A Construction Site

"That's the biggest hole I've ever seen!" "How do they get that big machine down there?" "Is that a steam shovel or a steam roller?" Visit a construction site. These days you can find them almost anywhere downtown, or look in a nearby neighborhood where sewer, roads or homes are under construction. The best time to visit is weekdays, avoiding lunch hours. Bring along ear plugs and a hardhat, and don't forget to come back again and again to watch the progress.

Puddle Walk
Your own neighborhood, country dirt roads, off-street bike paths.
Hours: Any day in Portland or the metro area from mid Sept.-June, especially June!

Put on your boots and raincoats. Grab your big umbrella and head out in search of the biggest and deepest puddles. Enjoy a cup of hot chocolate by a toasty fire on your return.

The Oaks Amusement Park
Ft. of SE Spokane St.
Portland, 236-5722   ($)

Built in 1905, Oaks Park is one of the oldest amusement parks in the country. Funky amusements rides will thrill the young and old. A miniature train will take you through the park. There is roller skating and an antique carousel. The park has places to picnic overlooking the Willamette.

OLD PORTLAND TOWN

There are many ways to explore downtown Portland. You will find some possibilities listed in various sections of this book. We have suggested art tours, museums, galleries and interesting shops and buildings. A whole other approach to getting to know our city involves learning some things about the past in order to understand and appreciate the present. In downtown Portland, children can see a wonderful juxtaposition of past and present.

We have included bits of historical trivia for you to share with your children as you explore the city. Hopefully, this information will make the past a little more lively and will perhaps pique your interest to explore our city's history more fully. Most important, we hope this will help develop in children an appreciation of and concern for the preservation of our links to the past.

Start your exploration by looking at the map of downtown Portland. Notice the angle of the streets as they cross Burnside. Streets south of SW Ankeny were laid out on Magnetic North. In 1845, streets north of Ankeny were laid out by Sea Captain John Couch on true North and the North Star. There is about a 20 degree difference between the true North and Magnetic North.

Notice that downtown the blocks are small and there are no alleys. The blocks were specifically laid out this way to provide for more corner lots, which were commercially more valuable. Without alleys, deliveries had to be made at the street level, and thus the elevator entrances in the sidewalk.

As you wander around the city, encourage children to develop the habit of looking up at the tops of the buildings. The real personality of older building is often above the ground floor. It is particularly fun to look for carvings of faces, gargoyles and animals. Often the carvings have symbolic meanings. For example, a lion's head means courage, a woman might represent liberty, and a pineapple hospitality.

As you drive along SW Front Avenue, between Ash and Oak Streets, notice the black holes by the windows at the backs of the buildings. These were for hinges for heavy steel shutters that were closed at night to help protect the buildings in case a neighboring building caught fire. Large sections of downtown Portland burned in 1872-73. A visit to the small museum in the central fire station at 55 SW Ash helps explain why fire was such a concern.

There was no electricity in Portland until 1889. It may be interesting to ask children to imagine living without electricity and how our lives and surroundings would be different. You can see some of these differences in the buildings downtown. Without electricity there were no elevators. Buildings were no more than three stories tall. (Additional floors were often added after electricity.) The New Market Theater, 1213 SW Ash, was the tallest building in town in 1872.

Large windows were necessary before electricity for both light and ventilation. Compare the building on the southwest corner of Third and Oak with the new Portland Building. Many buildings also were built with open areas in the center. This was designed to provide both natural light and air to the interior sections of the buildings. It also was often the location for outhouses!

Notice the buildings with wide doorways and arches. While merely decorative now, these were originally designed to allow horses and wagons to enter. Imagine the former Old Spaghetti Factory at 126 SW Second as a livery stable with horses below and hay stored upstairs. Farm wagons drove right into the New Market Theater building.

Portland has the largest number of cast iron buildings still in existence west of the Mississippi. Many of these buildings have been carefully renovated. Take a magnet to discover which of these buildings' pillars are real cast iron and which are non-metal copies made during restoration. A good area for this test is NW First., from Ankeny to Oak.

Prior to paving, the streets of Portland were dirt and with our rainy climate, mostly mud. Wooden planks were put down to keep the wagons from sinking into the mud. If you look into a hole at a street construction site in the Old Town area, you may be able to see the layer of paving stones that were used. The stones are still on the surface of the streets around the Skidmore fountain.

In many residential sections of town, as well as downtown, the corner curbs still have the metal rim that protected them from being broken down by wagon wheels. The rings embedded in the curbs around town were originally designed as tethers for horses.

Looking across Tom McCall Waterfront Park, it is difficult to imagine the bustling, rowdy waterfront of old Portland. In the 1890's there would have been dozens of masted ships and schooners tied up from all over the world. At one time Portland was even investigated by international maritime agencies because it was considered a "sin city".

There are still many interesting reminders of our seafaring heritage. When the large sailing ships came to Portland they were often loaded with ballast (rocks and sand) which they dumped when they picked up cargo. There are a number of buildings in the downtown area whose foundations are built from the ballast dumped by these ships. One example of this is the basement level of the Yamhill Market, 110 SW Yamhill. Here you can see an exposed irregular stone foundation wall built from ballast brought in by the masted sailing ships.

Another romanticized reminder of those days are the tunnels that run from buildings along Front, First, and Second Streets to the water's edge. The tunnels were used to transport merchandise from the ships to the stores and warehouses lining the waterfront. They were also used for less legal activities such as to shanghai seaman and as opium dens!

The Elephant and Castle (1886) Building, 201 SW Washington, has five tunnels leading to the harbor wall. The Bishop's House (1879) 223 SW Stark, has a tunnel that ends at the harbor wall and a tunnel that ends at the old police station at SW Second and Oak. The tunnels are unsafe now and most of them have been bricked up. There are no tunnels open to the public.

Before dams controlled the river level, Portland was also subject to periodic floods. The Hazeltine Building at 133 SW Pine has markers that show the water levels during the floods of 1892 and 1948.

There are many good walking tours of downtown for children. (see **RESOURCES**). A visit to the Architectural Preservation Gallery at 26 NW Second Street, is a must. Not only are there exhibits, but self-conducted walking tour guides and information about Portland neighborhoods and historic buildings.

Of Special Interest

• Dekum Building (1892), Third and Washington. Notice all the entrances to the building are different. There are 308 faces carved around and above the doorways.
• Le Panier, 71 SW Second. Above doorway delightful grinning faces.
• Guild Theater Building. Alder, between Sixth and Seventh. Bust of famous composers.

• New Market Theater
  213 SW Ash

Count the chimneys! At one time there were stoves for each of the farmer's market stalls. The present chimneys are not functional.

Look at the display on the upper level. It has information about the early days of the building and some artifacts found during restoration.

See the stencils along the first floor ceiling. One is an original from which the others were copied. Can you find it?

Note the size of the doors. Big enough for a farm wagon to drive through!

Use a magnet on the pillars. Some are original cast iron, others copies.

URBAN NEIGHBORHOODS

One of the many things that makes Portland a livable city are its urban neighborhoods. Many neighborhoods were originally villages with their own central business districts and school systems.

Unable, or unwilling, to compete with shopping centers and large department stores, some of these areas have cultivated small specialty shops and restaurants while retaining some of the flavor of the original village. We have included those areas that seem to offer the most to see and do for children and adults.

As you walk around, visualize these neighborhoods when they were small villages with wooden sidewalks and unpaved (usually muddy) streets, and connected to Portland by ferryboat or streetcar.

Sellwood

Sellwood was named for the Rev. John Sellwood, who settled the area in 1856. It was incorporated as a village in

1887. A furniture company and lumber mills were its major industries. Sellwood was connected with the communities of Portland, East Portland and Albina by a ferryboat that operated from the end of Spokane Street. Streetcars connected it to Portland in 1892, and it quickly became the main junction with the then interurban car lines and the electric railroad to Oregon City. See the old stone car barns, built in 1905, at 8856 SE 13th.

The area on SE 13th, between Ochoco and Tacoma, is the old commercial section. The area is now known for its antique shops. Southeast 13th, between Miller and Umatilla, makes the most interesting walking, though there are shops scattered all along 13th.

Places to visit in Sellwood are: The oldest building (1885-1887) at 1326 SE Tenino; Oaks Park; Oaks Bottom; and Sellwood Park. (See the index for more information.)

St. Johns

St. Johns was one of the first river towns on the Willamette. James John filed the plat in Oregon City in 1852. For a period of time, St. Johns was a part of the city of Albina. In separating from Albina, it became an incorporated village. In 1915, St. Johns joined Portland. Despite its long association with Portland, its geographic isolation on a peninsula between the Willamette and Columbia rivers, has helped it maintain a very separate identity.

Redevelopment projects in the downtown area of St. Johns have helped create a lovely small square. The St. Johns City Hall and the St. Johns Bridge are national historic landmarks. Worth further exploration are the St. Johns Bridge, Pier Park and Cathedral Park. (See index for more information.)

Multnomah

The Multnomah neighborhood is an example of a community that grew as a result of the railroad connections with Portland.

The area was originally settled in 1852, and up to 1890, it was mostly heavily wooded farmland, with the beginnings of a dairy industry. The Oregon Electric Railway Co., which reached Multnomah in 1907, placed the village 15 minutes from downtown. Between 1907-17, the area experienced tremendous growth. The commercial district of Multnomah retains some of the flavor of a friendly rural village. As in Sellwood, Multnomah has many antique and curio shops. The Raz dairy farm, still operated by descendants of early Swiss dairy farmers, is only moments away from downtown Multnomah.

Hawthorne Boulevard

Originally know as "U Street", Hawthorne Boulevard was named "Asylum Avenue" after the Oregon Hospital for the Insane located on what is now SE 10th and Salmon. When the state hospital moved to Salem in 1883, the name was considered inappropriate, and the street was renamed in honor of the founder of the institution, Dr. J.C. Hawthorne.

Present day Hawthorne Street, between about SE 34th and 39th, has developed into an interesting and diverse commercial district. There are thrift stores, antique stores, used book stores, restaurants, and bakeries.

Northwest

While several of the other neighborhoods we mention convey the sense of a small town, Northwest 21st and 23rd Avenues, between Burnside and Thurman, are urban in spirit. There are more brick apartment buildings here than elsewhere in Portland and the population is the densest. Northwest has a diversity of people and style found in large city neighborhoods.

There are numerous small specialty shops and ethnic restaurants along both 21st and 23rd Street.

Northwest is one of Portland's oldest residential areas, with buildings dating back to Captain John Couch who claimed the area in 1885. One example still standing is the small wood frame building at 2061 NW Hoyt. This was originally built as a school for the Couch children and their neighbors. Many of the large old neighborhood homes have been or are being renovated. Stroll down NW Hoyt, at 17th Street, and see the beautifully restored Victorians.

GARBAGE TOUR

The Metro area throws out more than 1,600 tons of garbage each day. Ever wonder where it all ends up? Local garbage haulers arrive weekly to dump your garbage into their truck and haul it off to be squeezed, crushed and pushed tightly together by a powerful automatic compressor. Your garbage, in its much reduced state, ends up at either the Clackamas Transfer/Recycling Center (CTRC) at 16101 SE 82 Dr. in Clackamas, or the St. Johns Landfill, 9363 N Columbia Blvd. Both facilities will be glad to give you and your group a tour. Contact Metro Solid Waste at 221-1646.

Garbage at the CTRC goes into a large pit that measures 150 feet long, by 40 feet across, by 12 feet deep. From there, gigantic semi-trailer trucks make hourly runs hauling garbage from the pit out to the St. Johns Landfill.

Officials say that more than 30 percent of the garbage we throw out daily could be recycled. Both the CTRC and St. Johns Landfill have rows of marked bins into which the public and haulers can drop the recyclable materials. There are also places to take yard trimmings where they can be ground into barkdust and other usable products.

For an activity, you and your kids can take your recyclable items to the the CTRC, the St. John's Landfill, and numerous centers throughout the Metro area. There are even companies that will buy your recyclable items, especially newspapers. For more information, call the Recycling Center Switchboard, 224-5555.

WATER TOUR

The city of Portland and surrounding Metro area gets its

water from the Bull Run Watershed, located on the Sandy River near Dodge Park. The watershed is a protected area of more than 600 square miles of forest lands. Water is collected and stored in several large lakes (reservoirs) located within the watershed area. From the lakes the water flows through "a screen house"where it is injected with chlorine and ammonia before the long trip to Portland. For a tour of the Bull Run Watershed area call 796-7459.

From the watershed, water is carried by gravity underground in large conduits. Around 162nd Avenue and Powell the water is diverted to several locations. Some of it goes to the Powell Butte Storage facility; some is sold and piped to other water companies; and the remaining water is carried to the three reservoirs on Mt. Tabor.

The Mt. Tabor reservoirs serve the east side of the Metro area. From Mt. Tabor, the water travels underground in a westerly direction, again in conduits, to two reservoirs in Washington Park. These reservoirs serve Portland's west side. From the reservoirs on the east and west side, water enters the city's water lines, bringing it to our homes and businesses. You might point out to your child the water meter at your home, and then show them the water bill. How many gallons does your family use a day? The Portland-Metro area uses 160 million gallons a day!

From Water To Sewage To Water Again

Young children often ask, "Where does the stuff that we put down the drains and toilets go?" The stuff (sewage) goes out from drains and toilets into city sewer collection pipes under our streets. It then flows by gravity to various trunk throughout the Metro area, most of it ending at the Columbia Boulevard Sewage Treatment Plant at 5001 N Columbia Blvd. More than 831 million pounds of sewage (99.5% water), flows daily through primary and secondary treatment programs. The primary treatment breaks up all solid materials with the use of settling tanks and skimmers. At the secondary treatment stage, micro-organisms are introduced to help remove pollutants. In the final stage, chlorine is added and the water flows out into the Columbia River.

The treatment of sewage has two recyclable benefits; gas and compost. During removal of pollutants, methane gas is produced, which goes to heat the plant. The gas is also sold to private companies. To make compost, the treatment plant refines the sludge not dissolved into a refined dry material which is then sold to a composting company. There it is mixed with sawdust and sold as compost to the public to be used in our yards and gardens.

For tours of the plant call 285-0205.

PARKS

You can hardly go wrong with Portland's parks. Our city parks have an international reputation. The parks listed represent a cross section of what is available. Some are great for big family picnics or simply because they are wild and woody. Other parks were included for interesting playground equipment or other special features.

Don't stop here but explore all of Portland's parks!

NORTH

Cathedral Park
N. Edison and Pittsburg, located under St. Johns Bridge on east side of Willamette River.

Called Cathedral Park because the arches of the St. Johns Bridge look like the soaring beams of a gothic cathedral. The park provides access to river swimming, fishing, and a public boat launch. Jazz concerts during the summer.

Kelley Point Park

Located at the confluence of the Columbia and Willamette Rivers, this is an excellent place to watch tugs at work and the large ships leaving and coming into port. There is a pleasant beach, paved walkways, picnic tables and grills for cooking. No playground equipment.
Directions: I-5 to Marine Drive exit. Go west past the Expo Center. Follow signs to Kelley Point Park.

Pier Park
North Seneca and St. Johns

A personal favorite, Pier Park (which is not on water as the name implies), contains the densest stand of old conifers of any Portland park. Enjoy the feel of the deep woods. On a hot summer day the sun is barely able to filter through the trees. Paved walkways ramble through the park making for easy walking any time of the year. The park is quiet on weekdays but tends to get busy on weekends with large picnic groups.

Directions: Highway 30, St. Helens Road, to St. Johns Bridge. Make left on Lombard, right on St. Johns Avenue, left on N. Seneca Street to the park. As you cross the St. Johns Bridge look to the left for the tops of a large stand of fir trees: that is Pier Park.

McCarthy Park
Swan Island

A wide, paved pathway offers a great place to ride a bike, take a stroll or push a stroller. You'll find that it is quiet and away from the traffic of the city. You will hear the river traffic on the Willamette River, ships loading and unloading and tugs hauling goods up and down the river. There are numerous benches for resting and picnicking. There is good access to the river's edge to throw rocks, dangle toes or throw in a line.

Directions: Take I-5 north to Swan Island exit. Take Channel Avenue and look for the sign, "McCarthy Park", near Ports of Call office complex. Park and walk to water's edge.

NORTHEAST

Peninsula Park
NE Portland Boulevard and Albina Street

Peninsula Park has a rose garden even larger than the Washington Park test gardens. There is a lovely gazebo overlooking the gardens. The playground equipment is extensive, with specific areas designed for older and younger children.

Fernhill Park
NE 37th and Ainsworth Street

A large, grassy park that for some reason seems to be seldom used. There are wonderful hills for rolling and running and open spaces for flying kites. There is minimal playground equipment.

Blue Lake Park   ($)
NE 223rd Street

Blue Lake Park is 185 acres of open and developed park space. The park borders on Blue Lake, a lovely small lake that has recently reopened to the public. There is a large swimming area. You can rent paddleboats and rowboats. There are places for fishing and feeding the ducks. Play structures are located in several areas, and there is a concession stand that opens at noon.

Note: Swim center additional charge, and only open when sunny and temperature above 72 degrees.

Directions: Located between Marine Drive and Sandy Boulevard, at 223rd, or take I-84 exit and follow Blue Lake signs north.

SOUTHEAST

Kenilworth
Holgate and SE 34th Street

Well maintained neighborhood park with first-class, new play structures (two areas), and a new wading pool. Good picnic area. Tennis courts.

Laurelhurst Park
SE 39th and Stark

A large, green hilly park with a lovely pond that is a favorite for feeding ducks year round. Playground is across the street.

Mt. Tabor Park
SE Salmon and 60th

Mt. Tabor is said to be the only extinct volcano inside the city limits in the United States. From the top of Mt. Tabor you can enjoy striking panoramic views of the city. The park also has good hiking and biking trails. The city reservoirs for Bull Run water are located here. There are also picnic and playground areas. (See Index)

Note: The road to the top is currently closed to vehicles Mondays-Thursdays. The park is a popular gathering place for teenagers on summer evenings, and the noise level reflects this popularity.

Sellwood Park
SE 7th and Miller

Pleasant picnic area. Usually ballgames in summer. Easy access to Oaks Bottom hiking trails.

Westmoreland Park
SE McLoughlin and Bybee

Crystal Springs Creek runs through the center of this large southeast Portland park. The stream forms two large ponds. One pond is always full of hungry ducks looking for a handout. The other, called the casting pond because it can be used for practice castfishing, is sometimes used for small paddle boats. The creek, as it travels between the two ponds and the casting pond, are ideal for toy boat sailing. A fun project would be to build some small boats with your children and take them there for launching.

Westmoreland is also a popular place for sports fans. On almost any day you can find baseball or soccer games. The lawn bowling association has built a clubhouse here and most summer weekends you can watch a game. (see **SPORTS**)

Directions: Go south on McLoughlin Boulevard and take Westmoreland Park exit.

Tideman Johnson Park
SE 37th and Tenino

One of Portland's most undeveloped parks. Actually a ravine that borders Johnson Creek, its appeal is the diverse vegetation, and a striking abundance of birds. Follow the slope down at the entrance to the park. Staying on the trail, you will cross Johnson Creek. This trail splits and the barkchip trail continues along the creek and past the backside of Eastmoreland Racquet Club. Trail ends at SE Tacoma and Berkley. Immediately before and after the bridge crossing Johnson Creek, there are trails leading into the undergrowth along the creek. There are many places to get to the water's edge. Fun for older children. (Younger children should stay on trails because of high undergrowth.)

Note: Entrance to park is steep. A word of caution: Johnson Creek is a swift running stream—treat it with respect.

Directions: Entrance to park at end of SE 37th Street, which is an overgrown and gutted unpaved street.

Johnson Creek Park
SE 21st and Clatsop

In this serene little park, Crystal Springs Creek flows into Johnson Creek. The two streams form a peninsula. As they flow together you can see the clean water of Crystal Springs Creek flow into and disappear in the more murky waters of Johnson Creek. There is a small bridge to cross. The water flows rapidly here, so keep hold of the small adventurous types.

Leach Botanical Garden
6704 SE 122nd Ave., 761-9503

Leach Botanical Garden is a unique botanical park, built over a period of 40 years by John and Lilla Leach. It is now open for the public to enjoy. The Leachs' searched the Northwest wilderness in the '20s and '30s for rare plants. The gardens, currently being restored by volunteers, reflect the Leachs' love of the Northwest and its plants.

This is a place for quiet walks. There is an old moss-covered stone cottage. Johnson Creek cuts through the property. Guided tours of the grounds are available, call 761-9503. There are no playground or picnic facilities.

Note: While in the area, take a few extra moments to cross a covered bridge. To get there, follow SE Foster Road to SE 134th, turn right on 134th by the fire station. The street becomes Durndorf Road. Follow the road a short distance to the Cedar Crossing Covered Bridge. There is parking on the other side if you would like to walk it.

St. Francis Park
SE 12th St. between Oak and Stark Streets

A privately maintained park. A man-made brick-lined stream meanders through the park, over a waterfall and empties into several pools for wading. There is a huge climbing structure with platforms and wonderful hills and mounds.

Note: There are no restrooms. The park appears to attract transients.

Crystal Springs Rhododendron Garden
On SE 28th across from Reed College

The six acres of 2,500 rhododendrons are ablaze with color from early spring through late summer. Easy walking trails wind across bridges and around the flowers and trees. A pond and stream formed by Crystal Springs Creek are full of ducks and waterfowl year round.

Note: No charge except on Mother's Day.

SOUTHWEST

Japanese Garden
356 SW Kingston St.
Portland, 223-1321, 223-4070
Hours: Daily 10-6, summer. Daily 10-4, winter

Leave the noise of the city and enter the serene world

of tea gardens, moon bridges, reflecting ponds, waterfalls and streams. The Japanese Garden, considered one of the most authentic outside Japan, includes five traditional gardens. The Pavilion in the Flat Garden is used for special events and Japanese dancing. Call for schedule. The Tea Garden has a ceremonial Tea House built in Japan in the ancient way with pegs instead of nails. The Sand and Stone Garden is the most abstract. It has no plants, just rocks on raked sand. Sit and listen to the sounds of waterfalls among the native mosses and ferns in the Natural Garden and walk the crooked bridge among irises in the Strolling Pond Garden.

This is not an excursion for a boisterous crowd, but a wonderful place for sharing quiet moments and conversations all year round.

Washington Park International Rose Test Garden
400 SW Kingston
Portland, 248-4302

Portland isn't called the Rose City for nothing, and here is one of the best places for views of roses and the city skyline. The Washington Park International Rose Test Garden, perched on a hillside in Washington Park, contains as many as 10,000 plants. While the greatest variety of color is usually mid- to late June, the gardeners claim the more brilliant color is in the fall. The Shakespeare Garden, next to the Rose Garden, is planted with flowers and shrubs mentioned in the playwright's works.

Bishop's Close, Elk Rock Garden
11800 SW Military Lane

Open Daily, year round.

Bishop's Close is a 13-acre estate and garden maintained by the Episcopal Diocese. There is easy walking through beautifully manicured gardens as well as areas of natural vegetation. The estate includes a grove of madrona trees, stream, ponds, and wonderful views looking down on the

Willamette River and Elk Rock Island. Look for the "hole in the hedge" entrance to the garden from the upper parking lot. This is a quiet place for quiet walks, talks, and thoughts.

Note: This is private property, but public access is allowed. There are no restrooms and picnicking is not allowed. Parking is limited.

Directions: Go south on Macadam, turn left on Military Road and immediately turn right on Military Lane. Garden at end of road.

Gabriel Park
SW 45th and Vermont

A large grassy park, Gabriel has good playground equipment, tennis courts and a picnic area. You can usually find a softball or soccer game to watch during the summer months. There is also a small forest area for walking.

Tryon Creek State Park
11321 SW Terwilliger Blvd.
Portland, 636-4550
Open: Daily, 8-4:30

The Tryon Creek Nature House is the place to start exploring yet another wonderful state park within Portland's city limits. The Nature House has displays, a library, and programs and classes for adults and children the year round. Within the park, there are more than 80 species of birds and small animals.

There are 8 miles of hiking trails, 3 1/2 miles of horse trails, and 3 miles of bike trails. There is handicap access on specific trails. This is a great place to hike and observe nature 12 months of the year.

Willamette Park   ⑤
SW Macadam and Nevada

Willamette Park borders the Willamette River and is a great place to watch boat traffic, especially small-class sailboat races in the evenings and on weekends. An excellent place for

kite flying because there is usually a steady breeze coming off the river.
Note: Weekend user fee.

METRO

Commonwealth/Foothills Park
SW Huntington Avenue
Beaverton

The two parks are separated by SW Huntington Avenue. Commonwealth Park has a large central pond with a paved walkway all around. Good for hot-wheels, tricycles and beginning bike riders. The ducks and geese are aggressive. An interesting marsh is located at one end.

Foothills Park has play equipment and trails leading up to a wooded hillside.
Directions: Sunset highway 26 to SW Cedar Hills Boulevard. Turn right on Butner Road. When you come to Huntington (between 123rd and 126th), turn left.

Jenkins Estate
Grabhorn Road, off 209th and Farmington Rd.
Beaverton, 642-3855

Now owned by Tualatin Hills Parks and Recreation, the 68-acre Jenkins Estate is a lovely place to walk, picnic and view the Tualatin Valley. There are primrose-lined paths that meander through the woods and across a small bridge. The house is frequently used for weddings and special events.
Directions: West on Farmington Road, 209th Street, make a left on Grabhorn Road. About 1/2 mile down Grabhorn you will see signs for Jenkins Estate.

Greenway Park
Beaverton

Located in Beaverton bordering Scholls Ferry Road on the south, and Hall Boulevard on the north. The park contains a great deal of open space with Fanno Creek running through the middle. There is a great variety of waterfowl and bird habitats. A well-paved bicycle path of over three miles meanders throughout the park with few hills. A perfect place to take a beginning cyclist, stroller, or big-wheeler. In fact, we think it would be a great place to roller skate. The path also travels across several wooden bridges over Fanno Creek and goes by five unusual playground structures and other sports facilities. Walking or cycling is the best way to enjoy the park.

Directions: Enter from Hall Boulevard and Greenway Street. The path is to the east of the Albertson store. You may also enter from Scholls Ferry Road, turning north into the Parkside business complex. The path is to the east.

George Rogers Park
South end of State Street in Lake Oswego

This is a four-star park. It has everything; swimming holes with sandy beaches, a small stream for wading, a small waterfall for sliding, baseball diamond, boat launch, tennis courts, and wonderful playground equipment. Good fishing spots can be found on the trails leading to Oswego Creek. See if you can find the large chimney which is what is left of the first iron smelter in Oregon.

You can hike/bike from George Rogers Park to Mary Young State Park, a distance of less than 5 miles along the Willamette River. Take the path through George Rogers Park to Old River Road. There are good views of Rock Island and fishing spots just a short climb down to the water's edge. Old River Road is very flat and traffic is light and slow. It is an easy and enjoyable trip for young cycle enthusiasts. Paths lead into Mary Young State Park from Old River Road.

Mary Young State Park
Pacific Highway, West Linn

Mary Young State Park has hiking and biking trails. There

is easy access to the Willamette River for fishing, boating and swimming.

Molalla River State Park (See RIDES)

VANCOUVER

Vancouver Lake Park
6 miles west off I-5 via Fourth Plain Blvd.
Vancouver, Washington

This is the largest lake in the Portland metropolitan area and is a site for a wide variety of water sports — sailing, swimming, skiing, canoeing, wind surfing and rafting. Boats are available to rent. Nicely landscaped, with large grassy areas for sunbathing and picnicking or hiking nature trails.

Esther Short Park
8th Street and Esther
Vancouver, Washington

The oldest public square in Washington state, this five-acre site has a number of unique features. A towering slide has left parents weak-kneed for generations. A railroad engine is planted in the middle of the park. Sculptures, victorian rose gardens, and the Slocum House, constructed in 1867, give a sense of the city's early culture.

Marine Park
South Portco Drive
Vancouver, Washington

Enjoy games and picnics on the lawn while in full view of the special play equipment. A giant wooden turtle is just right for climbing into and onto. Down the road are boat ramps and a sandy beach. Watch the activity on the Columbia River and comb the beach for treasure.

Special Features

Following is a list of wading pools, swimming pools, and infant swings. Call Portland Parks and Recreation for specific information about park equipment. 796-5193.

Infant Swings

Albert Kelly	Montavilla
Fernhill	Normandale
Glenhaven	Peninsula
Hancock	Rose City Playgound
Lair Hill	Sellwood
Laurelhurst	Wellington

Wading Pools:

Alberta	McKenna
Arbor Lodge	Montavilla
Berkley	Mt. Scott
Brooklyn	Normandale
Clinton	Oregon
Columbia	Overlook
Creston	Peninsula
Essex	Pier
Farragut	Powell
Fernhill	Rose City Playground
Glenhaven	St. Johns
Grant	Summers
Harrison	Wallace
Irving	Wellington
Kenilworth	Westmoreland
Lair Hill	Wilshire
Laurelhurst	Woodstock
Lents	

Swimming Pools located at:

Abernathy	2421 SE Orange
Buckman School	320 SE 16th*
Columbia	7701 N Chautauqua*
Couch	2033 NW Glisan*
Creston	4454 SE Powell
Dishman CC	77 NE Knott
Grant	2300 NE 33rd
Montavilla CC	8219 NE Glisan
Mount Scott CC	5530 SE 72nd
Peninsula CC	6400 N Albina
Pier	9341 N St. Johns
Sellwood	SE 7th & Miller
Wilson High School	1511 SW Vermont
Woodlawn	NE 13th & Dekum

*Indoor Pool

Trails and Paths Within City Parks

Forest Park	46 miles
Gabriel	.71 mile
Hoyt Arboretum	8 miles
Japanese Gardens	.5 mile
Kelley Point Park	.6 mile
Marquam Hill Nature Pk.	4 miles
Marshall	1.49 miles
Montavilla	.4 mile
Mt. Tabor	3.75 miles
Pier Park	1.2 miles
Pittock Mansion & acres	.7 mile
Plaza Blocks	.4 mile
Terwilliger	3.5 miles
Washington Park	1 mile
Himes Park	1.35 miles
Madrona	.41 miles
McCarthy Park	.5 mile

SPORTS

Grab your hat, horn, whistle, popcorn, pompom, and catch a game in a Portland park or rink. No charge to watch some good competition. For more information on sports and recreational activities call:

Portland Bureau Parks and Recreation — 796-5150
Recreation For Disabled Citizens — 248-4328
Tualatin Hills Parks and Recreation — 645-6433
Portland Community Schools — 796-5123

Specific rinks or sports facilities also post activities. And don't forget your local high school athletic events.

SPECTATOR SPORTS

Lawn Bowling
Westmoreland Park
Season: Usually opening ceremonies early April through the fall as weather permits.

The Lawn Bowling Association has built a clubhouse and given it to the Park Bureau. There is usually an enthusiastic participant there to explain the game to interested observers.

Rugby
East Delta Park

Spirited matches are played throughout the year.

Lacrosse
East Delta Park
Season: Spring, February through June; Fall, September through November.

On the last weekend in April. 32 teams from throughout the Northwest compete for a championship.

Soccer
East Delta and other area parks
Season: Summer, July through August; Winter: September through April.

Leagues range in age from 6 to over 30 and in skills from rank beginners to almost semi-pro.

Basketball
Irving Park and other area parks during summer.

Archery

These locations offer safe places to practice. Bales of hay are provided. Bring your own equipment and targets.

Washington Park
Blue Lake Park
Portland Community College
East Delta Park

Baseball/Softball
Almost any city park in the spring and summer.

Amateur Hockey

Portland Amateur Hockey runs September through April. Summer season at Valley Ice Arena. Call ice rink for specific schedules. There is usually a charge for special events, otherwise games are free. Dress for cool temperatures.

Valley Ice Arena
9250 Beaverton Hillsdale Hwy.
Valley Plaza, 297-2521

Lloyd Center Ice Pavilion
960 Lloyd Center, 288-6073
PeeWee Hockey

Silver Skates
1210 NE 102nd, 255-4644

RECREATIONAL SPORTS

Ice Skating $

Clackamas Town Center
12000 SE 82nd, 654-7733

Lloyd Center Ice Pavilion
960 Lloyd Center, 288-6073

Silver Skate Ice & Roller Rink
1210 NE 102nd, 255-4644

Valley Ice Arena
9250 Beaverton Hillsdale Hwy., 297-2521

Roller Skating $

City sidewalks, Tom McCall Waterfront Park, Greenway Park and city reservoirs in Washington Park and Mt. Tabor.

Oaks Park Roller Rink
Ft. of SE Spokane, 236-5722

One of the oldest and largest roller rinks. It is part of Portland family traditions.

Mt. Scott Roller Rink
5530 SE 72nd., 774-2215

A city owned rink, this is one of the best buys in town at only 25 cents an hour, including skate rental.

For other roller skating rinks, check the Yellow Pages. Most rinks will adjust the speed of skates for young children.

KITE FLYING

Most of the larger city parks have open areas free of kite-eating trees and wires. Particularly good ones are:

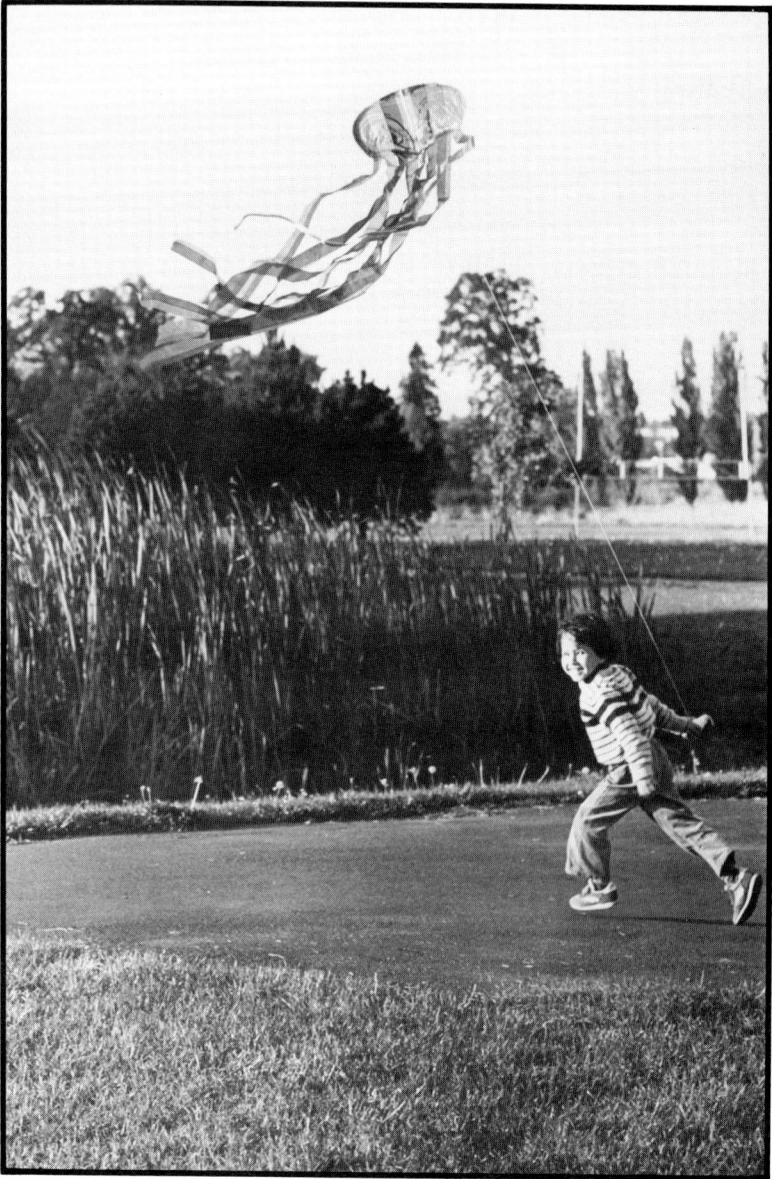

Fernhill — NE 37th & Ainsworth
Gabriel — SW 45th & Vermont
Tom McCall Waterfront Park — SW Front
Willamette Park — SW Macadam & Nevada

Remote Controlled Airplanes

There are almost always enthusiasts flying elaborate remote controlled airplanes at East Delta Park, weekends year round.

Boating

To sail homemade boats, try Westmoreland Park ponds and stream and Lewis & Clark College Reflecting Pool.

To watch sailboats, go to Willamette Park, the Columbia River, (off Marine Drive), and the Sailing Center, foot of SE Marion in front of Salty's Restaurant.

Fishing

Remember, to fish in Oregon, the adult accompanying a child under 12 must have a license even if they are not fishing. Anyone older than 12 must have a license in order to fish.

Columbia Slough
Columbia Road to Alderwood Road, turn on to Cornfoot Road. There are many places to park. Look for bridges over slough.

George Rogers Park — Lake Oswego

Willamette Park — SW Macadam & Nevada

Cathedral Park — N Edison and Pittsburg. Handicap access for fishing.

Columbia River - Along Marine Drive

There are casting lessons for kids in Westmoreland Park during the summer. Check with Parks Bureau for more information.

Hydrotubes/Water Slides $

Washington Square, Eastport Plaza, Jantzen Beach Center.

PROFESSIONAL SPORTS

Basketball — Portland Trail Blazers
700 NE Multnomah, 234-9291 $
Season: October 30 through April. Home games played at
Memorial Coliseum.

Baseball — Portland Beavers
1205 SW 18th, 223-2837 $
Season: April through August

Farm club of the Philadelphia Phillies. Practices at Civic
Stadium are open to the public prior to game time. Call for
more information. Various local businesses sponsor special
kids' days with ticket discounts and giveaways.

Hockey — Portland Winter Hawks
1401 N Wheeler, 238-6366 $
Season: October through mid-March

Practices open to public seven days a week, when in
town. 10 am at Silver Skates Ice and Roller Rink. The Winter
Hawks play at the Memorial Coliseum, and, usually, discount
tickets are available from area merchants.

Portland Meadows — Thoroughbred Horse Racing
1001 N Schmeer Road, 285-9144 $
Season: End of October through early April.

Children allowed only for daytime racing. Call the public
relations office for stable tours and information about morning workouts.

Multnomah Kennel Club—Greyhound Racing
NE 223 Road and Glisan
Fairview, 667-7700
Season: End of April to end of August.

$ ⃝

Children under 12 allowed only for daytime racing. There
is a paddock area where you can watch the dogs exercise.

Vehicle Racing

Portland International Raceway
West Delta Park, 285-6635
Season: Usually early spring to late fall.

$ ⃝

Handicap seating available. Call ahead. Call for schedule
of events. Some of the regular events at P.I.R. include: Bicycle racing, BMX, Drag racing, Go-Kart racing, Midget Car racing, Moto-Cross racing, 4-Wheel Mudarama, and CART Races.

Portland Speedway
9727 N Union Ave, 285-2883

$ ⃝

Call for schedule of events. Oval track. Primarily stock
car races and demolition derbys.

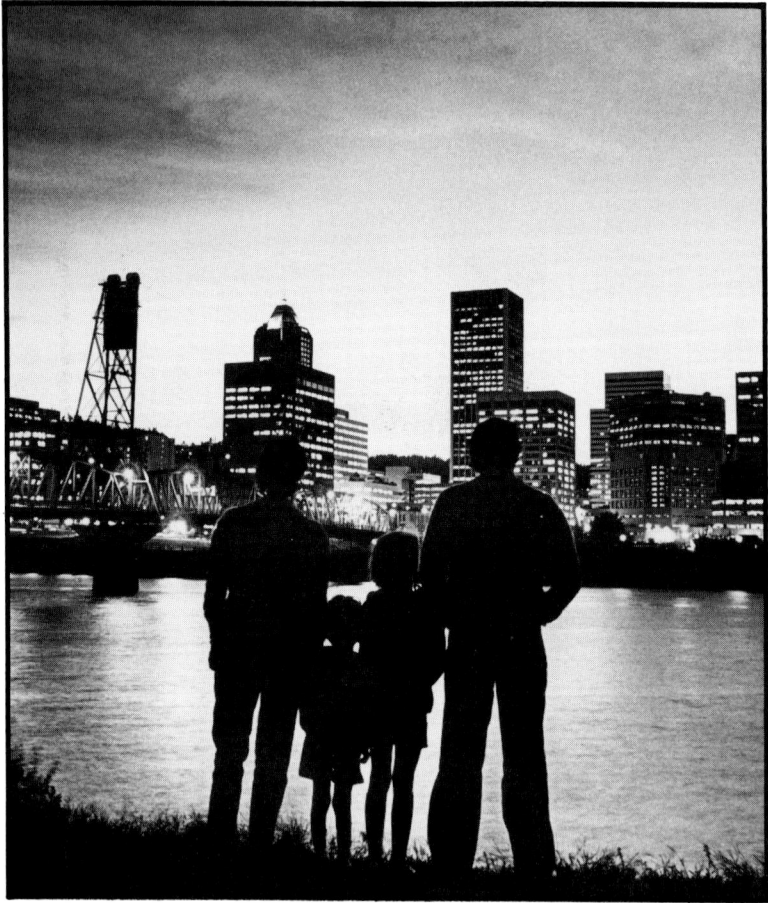

VIEWS

Portland is blessed with an abundance of breathtaking views that offer a variety of appealing experiences to a growing child, from its beautiful bridges and forested hilltops to modern skyscrapers (so high you can almost touch the clouds), down to the fascinating activities of two rivers. Tugs, barges and foreign tankers ply up and down the Willamette and Columbia Rivers providing splendid observations of a busy port city.

Why not take a break on a gray, cloudy day to find a hilltop to storm-watch, as the clouds roll in and out again. Return to the same spot in different kinds of weather—and Portland certainly offers a variety—to observe all the changes. Ask your child to locate your home, or a friend's, from various hilltops in the city. Sometime spend a quiet time up with the eagles—making pictures out of the big puffy clouds! Remember to include a city map to point out familar landmarks. Bring your binoculars.

Ross Island Bridge
SE Powell Blvd.

Park off Powell, on the east side of the river and walk along the sidewalk on the north side of the bridge. The bridge offers great views of Ross Island Sand and Gravel and Zidell's, a salvage plant. Observe river traffic from a bird's eye view. **Note:** An adventure walk for older children. Stay on the sidewalk and avoid rush hour traffic.

St. Johns Bridge
N. Philadelphia

One of Portland's most beaufiful bridges. A national historical landmark. Park on the east side and walk across the north side of the bridge. From this gothic structure you have a helicopter high look at much of the modern Port of Portland. You can see the unloading of Japanese cars. Portland is the main port of entry for Toyota Motor Co. Lots of Toyotas — count them! See other ships load and unload their cargo. **Note:** An adventure walk for older children. Stay on the sidewalk and avoid rush hour traffic, although traffic is generally much lighter in this area of the city.

Overlook View Point
North Portland
Off Overlook Boulevard, take N. Skidmore Court or Skidmore Terrace. Each street deadends, overlooking the Willamette river.

Park and walk out across the grassy area to see the terrific view. There is a single park bench and old apple tree to sit under. Below, you can see and hear the activity of the Union Pacific Rail Yards and river traffic from the Fremont Bridge to the St. Johns Bridge. A pleasant place to picnic and enjoy the sun or, on rainy days, to watch the storms roll in over the West Hills.

Note: This view is from a very high cliff with a sharp drop off with no fence so you need to watch little ones very carefully.

University of Portland
5000 N Willamette Ave.

Enter the college entrance and head toward the river. Walk behind the cluster of old buildings. This is the same lookout point from which the Lewis and Clark Expedition once viewed the river.

NE Marine Drive
From Gantenbein to Airport Way
Take Marine Drive east to Gantenbein; turn left to Bridgeton.

Many small and large boats are moored on the Columbia River. Most of the moorages are private, but some allow you to walk down to get a closer look at the boats. At Bridgeton, turn right and head east to Marine Drive. Continue along Marine Drive where there are numerous off-road parking spaces. View the river traffic of barges, sailboats, speed boats, wind surfers, and also the landing and taking off of both commercial and private aircraft, and at times, the Air National Guard or Air Force. An exciting street for a long, cloudy, winter day or to enjoy the cool breeze on a hot summer day. There are even snack vans parked near 33rd Avenue and opposite Portland International Airport.

Rocky Butte
Northeast Portland
Northeast 92nd Avenue to Rocky Butte Road on the south approach, or on the north side of the Butte, take 91st Avenue which winds around Judson Baptist College, with its stately white buildings and grounds. Either approach leads to the top by Rocky Butte Road.

On the top you can see all the large mountain peaks on a clear day: Mount St. Helens, Mount Hood, Mount Rainier, Mount Adams, Mount Jefferson. Seventy-four volcanoes are believed to have once been active in the area. More than a million years ago, of course! See if you can identify the mountain peaks. You'll be able to see the Columbia River and a bit of the Gorge and Larch Mountain. The Portland airport is also visable, affording a great view of planes approaching the airport. Looking west you'll spot the downtown city skyline.

Mt. Tabor
There are several entrances to the park. Some are only open to vehicles on weekends. Take SE 60th, and turn east on Salmon or Harrison. At the Salmon Street entrance is an

unobstructed view of the southeast Portland area.

Further in the park, you'll wind around to the top where you have a greater view to the west and on the other side of the mountain to the east. At the top you'll find the sculpture of Harvey Scott by Gutzon Borglum, who also did Mount Rushmore.

First Interstate Bank
1300 SW Fifth Ave.

There is a public restaurant with a panoramic view to the west. A second restaurant on the 28th floor, presents a view to the northeast. Not recommended for those with acrophobia!

Hilton Hotel
921 SW Sixth Ave.

A washroom with a view! The lookout from the men's or women's 23rd floor washrooms is breathtaking. Remember that this is a hotel with guests who do not wish to be disturbed by a large group of children. Enter quietly.

SW Vista Street Bridge
Spanning SW Jefferson Street

Begin on Vista Street at SW Burnside, continue up the hill to the bridge. Park on the north side and walk across. Great view of downtown with skyscrapers at your fingertips. Note the beautiful light fixtures along the bridge. A city neighborhood bridge restoration project is under way.

Pioneer Court House
Between Fifth and Sixth Avenue and Yamhill and Morrison

Except during the busiest hours, security guards will gladly take you up to the cupola on top of the building where you can rub noses with some of Portland's buildings and get a bird's eye view of the new exciting Pioneer Square across the street. Also, next to each window is an old photograph or drawing depicting the way it looked if you had stood at that same window more than a hundred years ago.

Washington Park Rose Test Gardens
SW Kingston

See one of the city's most popular and photographed views. Everyone takes visitors here to show off our city. The city sponsors a free summer performing arts series here and it's a real treat to enjoy a summer concert with the backdrop of the Portland skyline looking east. As the sun sets, the buildings begin to glow.

Council Crest Park
SW Greenway Avenue

A wonderful place to watch the clouds, a good storm, or to create pictures out of clouds or spaces in between. Good view to both the east—with the city skyscrapers—as well as a view of the Tualatin Valley. You will find here Fred Littman's sculpture "Joy", a Portland landmark.

SW Fairmont to SW Humphrey and back to Fairmont

Up in the West Hills of Portland, you will find that these streets all connect to give a panoramic view of the city and metro area. (see **METRO TRIVIA**)

Pittock Mansion (see MUSEUMS)

East Esplanade (see WALKS)

ARTS

Portland's first commissioned art work for the public was the Skidmore Fountain by Olin Warner, done in 1888. The city wanted a place where both man and horse could drink!

Works of art are created for many reasons and appreciated for just as many. We have included a variety of works—from sculptures (sometimes called statues), murals, and fountains. These pieces are not only for your enjoyment, but to serve as a visual and esthetic stimulation, to create a love and appreciation for the great art found right here in our community.

As parents, guardians and educators of children, it is our responsibility to develop a discerning eye to the art surrounding us daily in our homes, neighborhoods and communities. Just as a young child freely manipulates clay, paint, or blocks into a wonderful art creation to eagerly show us—we can quickly encourage and build on those experiences. Or we can place limitations and squelch those freedoms. Art needs our support at home and in the community.

This tour was developed to share with a child. Now go out and see the art, point it out, share it, enjoy the beauty it brings to us all!!

Some good advice, particularly for children, before you start:

- Use walk lights and pedestrian crosswalks.
- Pause often to enjoy a refreshing drink from the famous bronze Benson drinking fountains scattered throughout the downtown area. They were designed by A.E. Doyle.

Our walk begins downtown, at the Justice Center, and takes you to Main Street, across Lownsdale Square to view the famous "Elk" traffic separator, then west for a stroll down the Transit Mall and a look at the many interesting sculptures.

The tour cuts through the U.S. National Bank Building, onto Sixth Avenue, back up to Main, past the new Performing Arts Center, over to the Historical Society and Portland Art Museum for a tour of the South Park Blocks and its newly widened walkways and ends at the delightful Ira Keller Fountain across from Civic Auditorium.

Begin at the Justice Center (1), designed by the Portland firm of Zimmer, Gunsul, and Frasca, located between Second and Third Avenue and SW Main and Madison. When entering on Third Avenue, you'll find the towering free-form sculptures of Walter Dusenberg, formed out of travertine. Looking up, you will discover the colorful mosaic ceiling tiles, formed with pieces of fused glass, by Liz Mapelli.

After entering, turn around to see the stained glass created by Ed Carpenter. This work is enjoyable from both the inside and outside. Located just behind the elevator is a mural of black history by Portland's artist Isaac Shamsud-Din and a sculpture of enameled steel by Portland artist Bonnie Bronson. Walk through to the Second Avenue entrance to find the Pacific Northwest Indian Eagle, carved in cedar by a Kwakitual Indian many years ago.

Leave the Justice Center by the Third Avenue door and head down to Main Street. Crossing over to Lownsdale Square, the famous "Elk" (2) will be on your right. It is one of Portland's earliest fountains, done by Roland Perry in 1900 out of bronze. Head back across the square to Fourth and Madison to the life-size replica of the Liberty Bell (3) in bronze, cast by the McShane Bell Foundry. Just across the street at City Hall, on the west side of Fourth, is the oldest work of art in Portland—a Petroglyph (4) of basalt, with carvings done by Oregon Country Indians, in 1500 A.D.

From here go to Fifth and Madison and start your walk down the Transit Mall. Listed here are the numbers of various art works to point out:

5. Portlandia (June 1985)—a 25-foot sculpture, copper on bronze, by Raymond Kaskey, on the controversial Portland

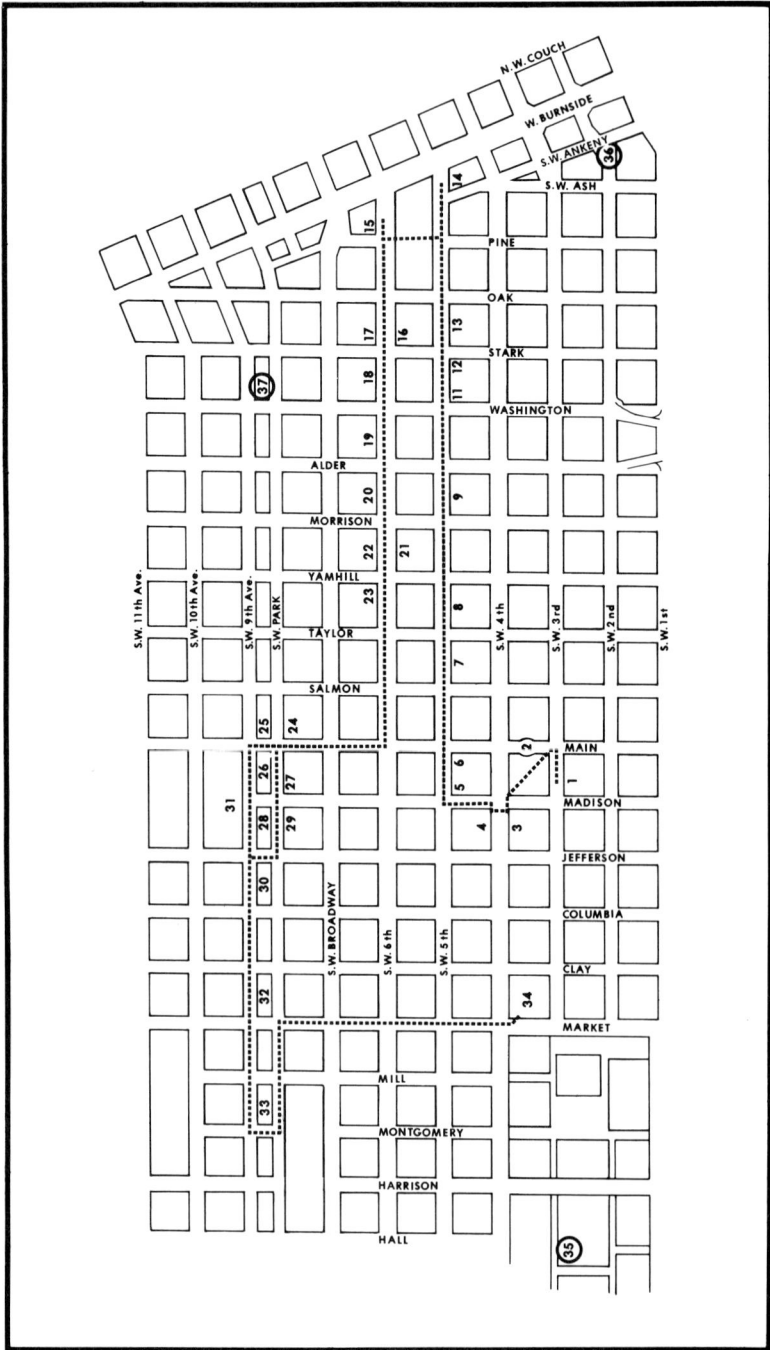

Building designed by Michael Graves. 1120 SW Fifth Ave.

6. Interlocking Forms—sculpture, Indiana limestone, by Don Wilson. A great place to climb and take a breather. Fifth, between Madison and Main.

7. The Guest—sculpture, marble, by Count Alexander Von Svoboda. It weights 17 tons. Fifth, between Salmon and Taylor.

8. Fountain—granite, by Carter, Hull, Nishita, McCulley, and Baxter. One of several fountains you will see by this firm. Stick your feet or hands in to test the temperature of the various pools of water. Fifth and Yamhill.

9. Cat in Repose—sculpture, Indiana limestone, by Kathleen Conchuratt. Fifth, between Alder and Morrison.

10. Thor—sculpture, copper on redwood, by Melvin Schuler. Representing the Scandinavian god of journeys and justice. Fifth and Washington.

11. Kvinneakt "Nude Woman"—sculpture, bronze, by Norman Taylor. Now famous for the "Expose Yourself to Art" poster. Fifth and Washington.

12. Forms Found in Nature and in the Tools of Men—sculpture, fountain of aluminum. Bridge, Beardles, and William Berkey. Fifth and Washington.

13. Steel sculpture by Bruce West. Great to knock on and hear the various tones. Fifth, Between Stark and Oak.

14. Fountain—steel and concrete. Carter and group (8). Take a walk behind the waterfall. Fifth and Ankeny.

Now cross the street and walk through the U.S. Bank Building to SW Sixth Avenue, and continue on Sixth to Main

15. Sculpture and Fountain—steel, by Lee Kelly. One of the best fountains for children to romp about—under, over and through water. Kelly has done several fountains. Called the "Golden Fountain" by my son. Sixth, between Pine and Oak.

16. Lions Heads—a quick look through the windows of the Hong Kong and Shanghai Bank. 300 SW Sixth. Big lions leer out at you.

17. Doors—sculpture, bronze relief, by Avard Fairbanks. Gigantic doors to the U.S. National Bank Building which is also a work of art. Doors have symbolic themes — a good opportunity for a guessing game using your imagination. The doors are similar in technique to Ghiberti's "Gates of Paradise" in Florence. The doors are at the Sixth and Broadway entrance and at the Stark Street entrance. They are visible only when the bank is closed.

18. Fountain — brick and granite. Carter group (8). Wonderful for going up or down on different levels. Sixth, between Washington and Stark.

19. Sculpture — aluminum, by Ivan Morrison. Variety of colors with little areas for tiny people to crawl through. Sixth between Washington & Alder.

20. Talos-2 — sculpture, bronze, by James Hansen. Representing a Greek warrior. Sixth between Alder & Morrison.

21. Historic Pioneer Courthouse. Offers an architectural contrast with the Justice Center. At Sixth Avenue entrance there are two caryatids of wood more than 15 feet tall. The entire building is done in rich woods with high, vaulted ceilings. On the Fifth Avenue side, ask a security guard to take you up in the elevator for a view from the cupola. (see **VIEWS**)

22. Pioneer Courthouse Square — brick and concrete with terra cotta columns, designed by the firm of Will Martin and Associates, 1984. Originally the site of Portland's first schoolhouse and later the Portland Hotel. Now a gathering place for people to meet, cool their feet in the fountain, enjoy a concert, look for names on bricks, or just people-watch.

23. Fountain — sculpture, aluminum and stone, by Robert Maki. Good place to have a leaf-floating race. When you walk by the fountain, you'll also notice that it creates an optical illusion. Sixth, between Yamhill and Taylor.

24. Performing Arts Center (in construction stage). New home for Portland Symphony. Between SW Broadway and Main.

Turn right off Broadway onto Main and walk to Park. Turn left on Park, for a tour of the South Park Blocks.

25. Rebecca at the Well — sculpture-fountain. Bronze and sand-

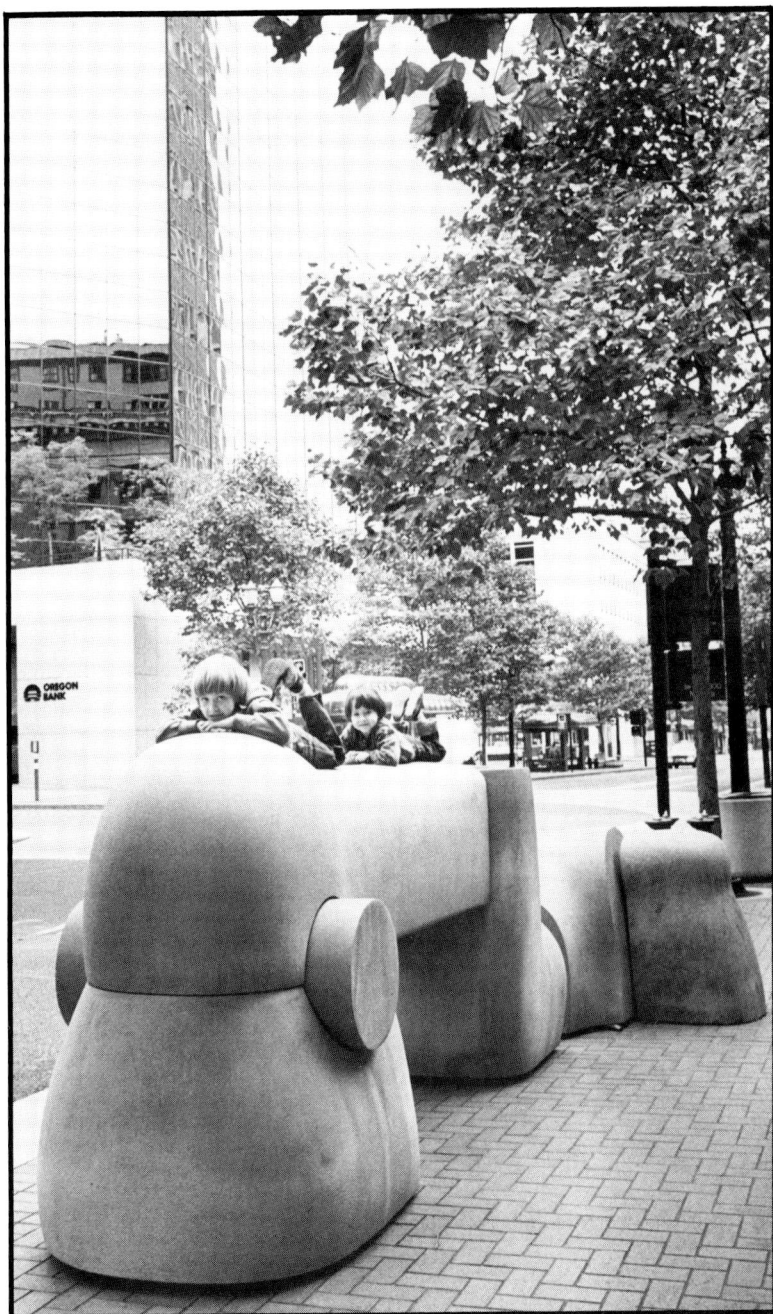

stone, by Olive Barrett and Carl Linde. Good place to discuss how water used to be drawn from a well. SW Park, between Salmon and Main.

26. Abraham Lincoln—sculpture, bronze, by George Waters. Lincoln in a somber mood—the sculptor stated that this was the Lincoln of the Civil War years. Park, between Main and Madison.

27. Windows—stained glass, by David Povey, at the First Congregational Church. Povey was a very talented glassworker who did scores of windows in both homes and churches in Portland's early days. Park and Madison.

28. Theodore Roosevelt, Rough Rider—sculpture, bronze, by Phimister Procter. It was commissioned in 1922 for $40,000. Between Jefferson and Madison.

29. Horse Cavalcade—1982 mural, paint on cinderblock. William Garnet. Looks like a backdrop for a Hollywood western. Park and Madison.

30. Sculpture—granite. By Steve Gillman. Interesting forms of white granite. Good for climbing on. The sculptor brought his stone to Oregon on a large truck from California.

31. Between Main and Jefferson, located in the courtyard of the Portland Art Museum, is the Evan H. Roberts Memorial Sculpture Mall. Displayed here are: a steel structure by Michihiro Kosuge; Barbara Hepworth's Dual Form in bronze; Lee Kelly's steel-Arlie; and two steel structures by Clement Meadmore and Richard Serra. You will also find a bronze relief of Rodin by Pierre Renoir.

32. Environmental Mosiac—granite, by Paul Sutinen. Park, between Market and Clay.

33. Farewell to Orpheus—sculpture, bronze, by Federic Littman. Park and Montgomery.

From here, head back downtown and turn east on Market Street. Walk down to Fourth Avenue to the Ira Keller Memorial Fountain (**34**) (Forecourt). Take a rest and cool your feet in the many streams of water. More than 13,000 gallons of water a minute cascade over the high concrete walls. Designed by

Angela Danadjieva for Lawrence Halprin. Third and Clay.
Now you are just a few blocks from the Justice Center, where you started.

BY CAR

There is still a great deal of art to be seen, but it is best reached by car.

In the downtown, there are three more exciting fountains to explore. The Lovejoy fountain (**35**), another fountain by Halprin and Associates, in the Portland Center off SW First and Hall, behind the Portland Center Plaza. The Skidmore Fountain (**36**) by Olin Warner at First and Ankeny was mentioned earlier.

O'Bryant Square (**37**) not only has a wonderful fountain to sit beside, but many fine concerts are performed here during the summer months. Designed by Danile, Mann, Johnson, and Mendendall, it is at SW Park and Washington.

Now off to discover some decorative murals in the downtown area.

• Bighorn Sheep — paint on concrete by Greg Brown. They even have shadows. SW Tenth, at Salmon.

• The Audience — paint on wood, by James Gardiner. 1530 SW Yamhill.

• The Rose — paint on concrete, by Jonathan Gibson. SW Thirteenth, at Washington.

NORTHWEST

• Figures and Phrases — chalk on concrete, by Tom Stefopoulos. The drawings were done in 1948 and have been preserved in relatively good condition. Located under the Lovejoy ramp to the Broadway Bridge at NW Twelfth. Surrounded by lots of old cobblestone streets.

• Butterfly — paint on brick, by Joe Erceg. NW First at Davis. Portland's own pointilist work of art.

SOUTHWEST

Washington Park is not only a beautiful park to be enjoyed by all, but it also contains numerous pieces of artwork to notice the next time you visit.

• The Frank Beach Memorial Fountain — at the Rose Test Garden, steel, by Lee Kelly and David Cotter. Beach nicknamed our city the "Rose City". The fountain is a delight to dance around, and in, for people of all ages.

There are numerous beautiful sculptures located in the Zoo. They are hands-on, climb-on sculptures for kids and adults.

• Bear and Nursing Cubs — marble, by Beniamino Bufano.
• Lion — bronze, by Phimister Procter.
• Sleeping Badger — serpentine by Tom Hardy.
• Totem Pole — by Chief Dan Lelooska.
• Follow the Park Street entrance in Washington Park to see the famous bronze sculpture of Sacajawea by Alice Cooper.

SOUTHEAST

• Sculpture — steel by Lee Kelly, Bonnie Bronson, and assisted by Duniway School students. Kids can do sculpture also! 7700 SW Reed College Place.
• Benjamin Franklin — sculpture, sandstone. A statue of that famous man at Franklin High School. 5405 SE Woodward.
• Harvey Scott — sculpture, bronze. Located at the top of Mt. Tabor, 60th, between Division and Yamhill. By Gutzon Borglum, who also sculpted the famous presidential faces at Mount Rushmore.
• The Crystal Pallets: Defense of Light — sculpture, glass by Richard Posner. The panes of etched glass with photos tell of remarkable events in our nation's political life. A must for political history students. Located at the Multnomah County Elections Building, SE Eleventh and Morrison.
• Buckman Neighborhood Mural — acrylic on cinderblock, by Geoffrey Clark and Buckman School students. Another display

of children's art. SE Twelfth and Morrison.

• Fountain—steel and brick by Bruce West. St. Francis Park, 1136 SE Oak.

ARTS

Portland is blessed with many fine and talented artists. We've included a sampling of schools and centers which are dedicated to encouraging and instructing in the various arts at all ages and levels of skills. Classes offered in fine arts, crafts, dance, music and theater. Call for a schedule of classes.

Oregon School of Arts and Crafts
8245 SW Barnes Rd.
Portland, 297-5544 $

Fine arts and crafts.

Pacific Northwest College of Art
1219 SW Park
Portland, 226-4391 $

Classes in fine arts and crafts.

Northwest Film Study Center
1219 SW Park
Portland, 221-1156 $

Classes in filmmaking, video, and photography.

Junior Civic Theater
1530 SW Yamhill
Portland, 226-3048 $

Classes in theater and production.

The Munchkins Too
918 SW Yamhill
Portland, 227-1927 $

Classes in dance.

The Oregon Academy
Beaverton, 644-5800   ($)
Tigard, 639-5388

Classes in dance, gymnastics.

Music Center
3350 SE Francis Street   ($)
Portland, 231-1955

Classes in voice, instrumental music, and appreciation.

Firehouse Theater
1436 SW Montgomery   ($)
Portland, 248-4737

Classes in performing arts.

Metro Dance Center
125 NE 82nd   ($)
Portland, 282-5061

Classes in dance.

YWCA
1111 SW 11th   ($)
Portland, 223-6281

Classes in dance and movement.

Multnomah Art Center
7688 SW Capital Hwy.   ($)
Portland, 248-4444

Classes in dance and art.

Children's Museum
3037 SW Second   ($)
Portland, 248-4587

Classes in music, art and crafts.

Performances and art works can be seen locally in numerous galleries and performing centers. Following is a list of galleries and theaters that we feel are of particular interest to children. Watch the newspaper and media for the schedule of exhibits and various performances of interest to children. Also check with your neighborhood high school for concerts and theater productions.

Tears of Joy Puppet Theatre
400 W Evergreen Blvd. ($)
Vancouver, 206-695-3050

Call for schedule of performances and puppet workshop.

Ladybug Theater
Washington Park Zoo, 228-5648 ($)

Weekly children's performances of fairy tales, often involving puppets.

New Rose Theater
904 SW Main Street ($)
Portland, 222-2487

Offers several youth performances a year.

Northwest Artists Workshop
522 NW 12th Ave. ($)
Portland, 228-0435

Offers numerous performances and exhibits to delight all ages.

Portland Youth Philharmonic
Portland, 223-5939 ($)

Has symphony and brass ensembles.

Contemporary Crafts Gallery
3934 SW Corbett ($)
Portland, 223-2654

Changing exhibits in ceramics, textiles, glass, wood and jewelry by Northwest artists. Participates in the "Artists in School" program.

Sunbow Gallery
206 SW Stark
Portland, 221-0258

Unusual and colorful collections of art works—in lots of shapes and sizes.

O'Connell Gallery
25 SW Salmon
Portland, 220-0330

Dancing mobiles hang from the ceiling—beautiful glass objects to collect the light in this very open setting.

Quintanas Gallery of Western Indian Art
139 NW Second Ave.
Portland, 223-1729

A collection of jewelry, paintings, sculptures and craft items made by Western Indians.

Folk Craft Gallery
302 SW First
Portland, 222-0063

Changing exhibits of folk art that always seem to enchant the young and old.

Photographic Image Gallery
208 SW First Ave.
Portland, 224-3543

A variety of photographs are on display here with lots of local representation.

MUSEUMS

Oregon Museum of Science and Industry, OMSI
4015 SW Canyon Rd.
Portland, 228-6674 ($)
Hours: Daily, 9 to 6 pm; Fridays until 8

Chock full of fascinating exhibits. Walk through a giant replica of a human heart! See the invisible woman. OMSI is a Portland favorite for both young and old. (See **RESOURCES**)
Directions: Zoo, OMSI exit off Highway 26 West.
Note: Planetarium and most exhibits on main floor. Call in advance for handicap access to lower level.

Kendall Planetarium
4015 SW Canyon Rd ($)
Portland, 228-7827
Hours: Daily, 9 to 6 pm, Multi-media laser light shows after 10 pm, summer and weekends.

Stellar attractions at all times.
Directions: Exit off Highway 26 West next to OMSI

Portland Art Museum
1219 SW Park ($)
Portland, 226-2811
Hours: Tues.-Sun., 12-5 pm; Friday until 10 pm; Free after 5 pm on Fridays.

Exhibits of special interest to children are the fine Northwest Coast Indian Art and the Asian galleries. Watch for touring exhibits. (See **ARTS**)

Portland Police Historical Museum
26 NW 2nd Ave.
Portland, 223-5771
Hours: Wed.-Fri., 10 to 3 pm; Sat.-Sun. 12-4 pm; Closed
November to April. To arrange group tours during winter
months, call 659-4672

Uniforms, photographs and memorabilia tell the
fascinating history of police work in Portland.

Children's Museum
3037 SW 2nd
Portland, 248-4587
Hours: Tues., Thurs., Fri., and Sat., 9-5; Wed., 9-4; Sun., 11-5 pm

A museum with exhibits especially for children to touch,
manipulate and experience. Beside the regular features—
tunnel and stuffed animals and doll displays—there are continuously changing exhibits. (See **RESOURCES**)

Oregon Historical Society
1230 SW Park
Portland, 222-1741
Hours: Mon.-Sat, 10-4:45 pm

The Oregon Historical Society's focus is on regional
history. Downstairs are rotating exhibits, while on the second
floor are dioramas on Indians of the Oregon country and life-
like displays of life on the Oregon Trail. The bookstore, near
the entrance, has one of the most complete collections in the
state of books about the Northwest, including children's books.
Note: Handicap access at the Broadway entrance.

Bybee-Howell House and Agricultural Museum
Sauvie Island, 232-1741, (Oregon Historical Society)
Hours: Wed.-Sun., 12-5 pm, June to Labor Day

The Children's Agricultural Museum is a collection of over
300 tools used for farming between 1840 and the 1920's, when
gas powered machines changed life on the farm. There are

films and photographs showing farm scenes from various periods. Children can climb on and touch some of the larger pieces of equipment.

The Bybee-Howell House was built in 1856 and has been restored and furnished for that period. Tours are regularly scheduled.

On the grounds of the homestead is an orchard with 100-year-old trees that is almost a "living museum" in itself. There are many unusual varieties of apples once grown in the Oregon Territory but no longer available.

The last weekend in September is the "wintering in" celebrations, with old cider presses, cider tasting, pioneer crafts and children's games.

Directions: Hwy. 30 to Sauvie Island, after bridge, turn left.

Fort Vancouver, Officer's Row, Grant Museum
1501 E Evergreen Blvd.
Vancouver, 206-696-7655
Hours: Daily, 9 to dusk.

Take a trip back in time at the Fort Vancouver National Park. As you enter the area you'll see, on your left, Officer's Row. The houses were constructed between 1849 and 1906 and served as homes for officers stationed at the military post. There is the Marshall home, built in 1886, which once housed General George C. Marshall and his family. There is also the Ulysses S. Grant House, which was built in 1849, and is the oldest house on Officer's Row. It is now a museum. Below Officer's Row is Vancouver Central Park, a large, open grassy park with an old fashioned bandshell. The park has a play structure, picnic area and many summer activities. You might want to take in the slide show at the Visitor's Center for historic background before going on to the Fort.

The Fort is a reconstruction of the 1825 Hudson's Bay Trading Post. Continuous guided tours are given, and during summer, guides are often dressed in period costumes. There are ongoing demonstratons of settlement crafts, including blacksmiths, bakers and weavers. Special children's programs are held at the Fort during summer. Call for information.

Directions: I-5 to Mill Plain exit. Turn right on Mill Plain and follow signs to Fort Vancouver.

Clark County Historical Museum
1511 Main St.
Vancouver, 206-695-4681
Hours: Tues.-Sun., 1-5 pm.

Board the Pullman car and pretend you're traveling cross-country. The ticket is free at this museum operated by the Fort Vancouver Historical Society. An entire room is devoted to railroad memorabilia. Other exhibits include a turn-of-the-century doctor's office, a country store, and print shop. Group tours available for a small fee.

Clackamas County Historical Museum
603 6th Street
Oregon City, 655-2866

The Historical Museum is in a 1908 house and is noted for its fine collection of Native American artifacts. There is also an entire room of antique dolls.

McLoughlin House
73 Center Steet
Oregon City, 656-5146
Hours: Tues.-Sat., 10-4:30 pm; Sunday, 1-4:30 pm.

The McLoughlin House was the retirement residence of Dr. John McLoughlin, an officer in the Hudson's Bay Company (see Fort Vancouver), founder of Oregon City and father of the Oregon Territory. The house was built in 1846, and was moved from Third and Main in 1909. Many of the furnishings and artifacts are from the McLoughlin family or date from his residence in the house. For groups and guided tours, call ahead.

Pittock Mansion
3229 NW Pittock Drive $
Portland, 248-4469
Hours: Wed.-Sun., 1-5 pm.

A French renaissance-style mansion built in 1909-1914 by Henry Pittock, founder of the Oregonian newspaper. The house is a showpiece of fine local craftsmanship. Several of the original craftsmen actually assisted in directing the restoration of the house in 1964, when the City of Portland purchased the estate to prevent it from being torn down. Tours are guided. The grounds are open daily and provide a spectacular view of the city and mountains. The Wildwood Trail crosses the property (see **WALKS**). The Gate House has recently been renovated and turned into a tea room serving light lunches. During the Christmas season the entire house is decorated.
Directions: Head west on Burnside. Signs indicate the turn for the Pittock Mansion.

Washington County Museum
17677 NW Springville Rd.
Portland, 645-6606
Hours: Mon.-Sat., 9-4:30 pm.

Exhibits trace the history of Washington County from early Tualatin Valley Indians (Atfalati), missionaries, and pioneer farmers, to the present impact of high tech companies. There is a picture display of old farmhouses that are still standing. The exhibits are self-guiding, but there are tours for groups. The museum also has a library for community and historical research.
Directions: Follow Hwy. 26 to 185th, turn right; follow signs to Washington County Museum. Located on the campus of Portland Community College, Rock Creek Campus.

Portland Carousel Museum
121 SW Salmon, Willamette Center
Hours: Open seven days a week

Next to the Willamette Carousel, the Portland Carousel Museum is scheduled to open soon. The museum will display a variety of wooden animals showing the enchantingly beautiful lost art form of the carousel. Exhibits will include the works of the major carvers, and a restoration area showing how carousels are repaired and restored. Changing displays are planned.

Architectural Preservation Gallery of Portland
26 NW Second Ave., 243-1923

A good first stop for those interested in learning something about Portland's architectural history. There are changing exhibits about Portland's historic homes and buildings, self-guided walking tours, neighborhood information, and a helpful staff.

TOURS

Most facilities included in these tours have special requirements. It is a must that you call in advance of your planned visit. Some places limit tours to a certain age and group size. Most tours are conducted weekdays, during regular business hours. Remember, people at the facilities are working at their jobs, so try not to cause disturbances. Some tours have individual guides who will direct your group. Consider your group's age, size, and interest before arranging a tour.

HOSPITAL

Most hospitals in the Metro area offer tours to groups, and to children entering for hospitalization. The tours generally include walks past or through various departments such as labs, pediatrics, emergency rooms, nurses' stations, and to view a hospital room. We have included a small sampling of the tours available. When calling to arrange a tour, ask for volunteer services.

Emanuel Hospital
2801 N Gantenbein
Portland, 280-3200

Puppet show and visit to the Lifeflight Helicopter Pad.

Portland Adventist Hospital
10123 SE Market
Portland, 251-6114

Classroom discussions stressing health education geared to specific age and understanding.

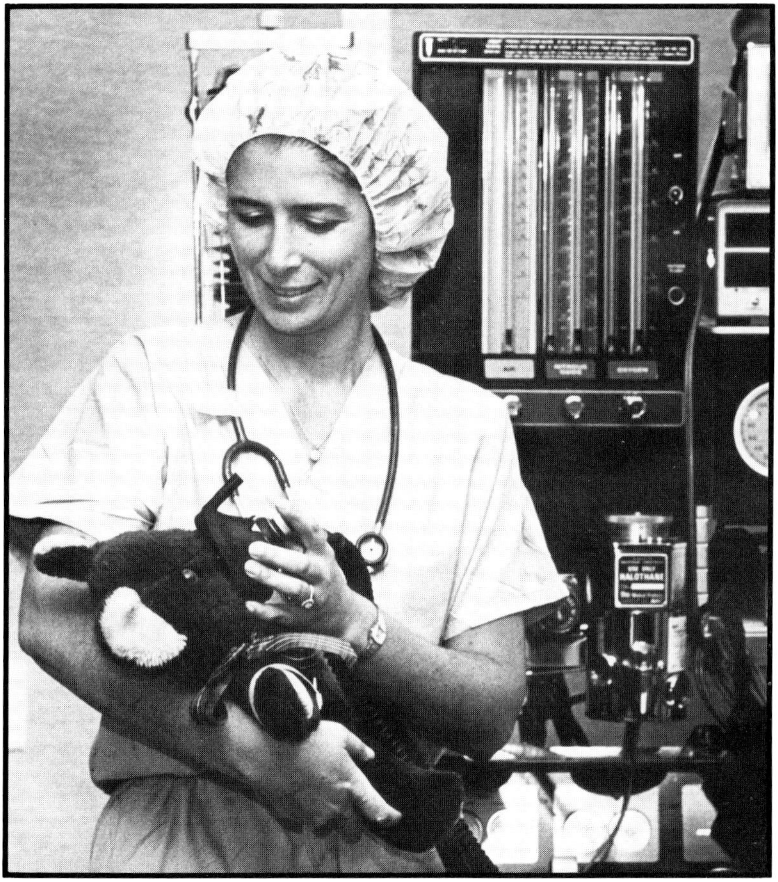

St. Vincent's Hospital
9205 SW Barnes Rd.
Portland, 297-4411

Special packet given at end of tour with health and safety items including "Mr. Yuk" stickers.

Providence Medical Center
4805 NE Glisan
Portland, 230-6069

FOOD TOURS

Skychef
7201 NE Alderwood
Portland, 249-4650
Monday-Friday, 1-4 pm.

See the entire preparation of food for air travel: from the sink, to the ovens, to the trucks that transport the food to the planes, for us to eat on our next flight.

Hoody
5555 SW 107th
Beaverton, 646-0555
Starting the first week in January. Tuesday and Thursday, 8 am-2:30 pm. Age: Third grade and up. Group size: Maximum 15. One hour.

See the processing of peanuts into peanut butter and syrups; packaging of both dry and roasted peanuts and sunflower seeds. Tours conducted February through May.

Steinfeld's Products
10001 N Rivergate Blvd.
Portland, 286-8241
Age: Sixth grade and up. Group size: small.

Watch the fine art of pickle making: From vines, to fermenting tanks, and into jars. This facility also makes relishes and sauerkraut.

Nabisco
100 NE Columbia Blvd.
Portland, 285-2571
Must call first week in October to schedule tour for that school year. Tuesdays and Thursdays. October-May. Age: Sixth grade and older. Group size: 25 maximum. Under two hours.

Production of crackers and cookies from the raw materials to the finished product.

Alpenrose Dairy
6149 SW Shattuck Rd.
Portland, 244-1133
Call the first week in September to set up a guided tour for that school year. Under two hours.

See the complete milk process from cow to carton. There is also a wonderful doll museum and an old car museum — open Sundays during summer. An animal petting area and pony rides are available on special occasions. During the Christmas season, see the Storybook Lane. Informal visits can be made to the dairy to attend the above activities as well as to stand at the window and watch the 4 pm milking of the cows.

Corno's
711 SE Union Ave.
Portland, 232-3157

A wholesale produce supplier for stores and restaurants in the Portland area, also a retail grocery store. One of Portland's most friendly stores with bins, cans and jars, full of tasty goodies. Tours are geared toward the special interest of the particular group. Don't forget to make an early morning visit to watch the unloading and loading of local produce. This area is nick-named "produce row".

Blue Bell Potato Chip
100 NE Farragut
Portland, 289-8851
Age: 12 and older; or one adult per child.

Follow the chip, from the potato through cleaning, peeling, slicing, cooking, and into the package!

Franz Bakery
340 NE Eleventh
Portland, 233-2191
Call at least a month ahead. Under two hours.

See flour mixing, baking, cutting, and packaging. A great place to enjoy baking smells—you even get to sample! You can stand at the window on 12th Avenue and watch part of the process.

Bread is baked 24 hours a day, Monday-Saturday, so just drive by and see if something is cooking. Don't visit on an empty stomach!

MEDIA TOURS

Several local stations have guided tours for school age children. We have included stations offering live audience programs under **EXCURSIONS**.

KATU Channel 2
2153 NE Sandy Blvd.
Portland, 231-4222
Call two weeks ahead. Age: 12 years and older. One hour.

KOIN Channel 6
222 SW Columbia
Portland, 243-6666
Monday-Friday, 11-1 pm. Age: Seventh grade and up.

KGW Channel 8 and Radio
1501 SW Jefferson
Portland, 226-5000
Call a month ahead. Age: Fourth grade and up. One hour.

KEX Radio
4949 SW Macadam
Portland, 225-1190
Call a week ahead. No age limit.

Chance to talk to the D-Jay.

The Oregonian
1320 SW Broadway
Portland, 221-8336
Call six weeks ahead. Age: 12 and older. Group size: Small groups only. Over 2 hours.

Newsroom and various departments of Portland's only daily newspaper. You can visit the editorial desks and the press plant where the paper is printed. You may get a copy hot off the press.

INDUSTRY TOURS

United States National Bank of Oregon
321 SW Sixth Ave.
Portland, 225-6378
Call a week ahead. Before the bank opens for business.

Tour the bank departments, the vault, and see the Rose Festival crown. The tour also includes some information on the architectural history of the building.

Union Railroad Station
800 NW Sixth St.
Portland, 241-4486
Call two weeks ahead. Less than one hour.

Visit the station and the railroad yards. Tour a lounge car and receive an engineer's cap.

Esco Corporation
2141 NW 25th Ave.
Portland, 228-2141.
Age: Junior High School and up. Group Size: Small groups only.

Note outside the world's largest cast steel sculpture, called "The Flogger" by Frederic Littman, a tribute to the steel industry. Inside, observe the melting down and pouring of metals. Hard hats and safety glasses are issued and wearing of old clothes is a must.

Crown Zellerbach — Saw Mill
Estacada, 630-7701
Call a week ahead. Call for directions and hours.

See the milling process from logs to lumber. There are logs floating in ponds and lots of big machines. Hard hats will be issued.

Portland International Airport
231-5000, ext. 422
Call two weeks ahead. Age: Third grade or older. Group size: Maximum 30. Monday-Friday, and weekends. One hour.

Tour includes walking through the entire airport with a guide to see all of the operations — except boarding a plane. There is also a slide presentation.

Port of Portland — Ship Yards
231-5000, ext. 208
Call ahead. Fills quickly.

Two types of tours. One tour is free and is only twice a week during the summer. It is for families with children of any age. You meet at 17th Avenue and NE Multnomah Street where you board a special chartered bus. The tour takes about two hours and you see the terminals, ship repair yards, and the airport.

The second tour is year-round and designed for a school group or organization. You must provide your own transportation and only one bus per tour. The tour is for third graders and up. You tour the same places as on the first tour, but you do not get off the bus or go to the airport.

There is also a traveling van program that visits classrooms with a slide presentation and program about port activities. Each year, the van travels to a different area. Ask your school principal to learn when the van is coming to your school.

National Weather Service
5420 NE Marine Dr.
Portland, 281-1911
Age: Fourth grade and up. Group size: Small groups are best.

There are rooms full of gauges, papers, recorders and screens that monitor the state's weather. You'll see machines that can measure the height of clouds, and one that counts the length of time that the sun shines. This is the first place to receive information of any pending natural disaster. Television and radio stations call here for hourly weather information. The facility welcomes informal visits of younger children, during regular business hours, if they are well supervised.

U.S. Post Office
715 NW Hoyt
Portland, 294-2200
Call ahead—never in December! Age: Over 10 years. Group size: Five or more. 90 minutes.

On a guided tour you'll see all the automatic equipment that moves the mail from your mailbox to its destination.

MISCELLANEOUS

Mounted Police Horse Stables
Portland, 289-8870

Take West Delta Park exit off I-5 and head for Expo Center—turn left on Force Avenue. Look for white gates on the right, and some green and yellow buildings. Turn right onto road. Call ahead and a mounted police officer will come to answer questions.

An interesting place to observe the care and training of the horses. Visit the barns and watch a horse get shaved and bathed.

Oregon Humane Society
1067 NE Columba Blvd.
Portland, 285-0641
Call two weeks ahead. Monday-Friday, 10-4 pm. 45 minutes.

Tour shows you through the facilities where you'll see the dog and cat pens, some barnyard animals, the cemetery, and the mausoleum. A film is shown on animal welfare, and a discussion held on the problem of over-population.

RIDES

Portland offers many ways for one to travel about. Whether you want to go by land, sea or air — up or down — or around and around, Portland has the ride designed for just what you had in mind.

CAROUSELS

Jantzen Beach Center Shopping Mall, 289-5555 ($)

The largest Parker carousel in the West, with 72 horses. Located inside the Mall area. Open daily, year-round.

Western Forestry Center, 228-1367 ($)

This 1914 outdoor carousel, with wooden lions and 54 horses, is open daily from noon until dusk during the summer months. After school begins, the carousel is open only on weekends, weather permitting.

Willamette Center
121 SW Salmon, 226-5757 ($)

An enclosed antique carousel in the heart of downtown Portland. Both the Willamette Center and Western Forestry carousels are privately owned by Portlander's Duane and Carol Perron, who are responsible for the preservation of this remarkably beautiful art form. This carousel was restored by community volunteers.

Oaks Amusement Park
Foot of SE Spokane, 236-5722 ($)

A 1920 Spillman, with two chariots and 64 animals in pairs. Open year round from noon to dusk. Winter—weekends only.

ELEVATORS

To elevate your spirits on those up and down days, try an elevator ride. You'll find the fastest, the sickest, the longest, and the best outdoor and indoor elevators. Just about any to fit your fancy!

Oregon City Municipal Elevator
Seventh Avenue and Main Street
Oregon City
7 am to 7 pm: Closed Sundays

Cross under railroad tracks through a cool tiled tunnel to the elevator. An operator controls the elevator and acts as guide. At the top you'll enter into a glass fish bowl effect. (My son called it the "space ship.") Here you have a panoramic view of the Willamette River south to the falls and north to the 205 Freeway.

200 Market Street ("The Black Box")

The elevator goes from the first to the 19th floor at a very fast and smooth pace. Rated the smoothest, but rather boring ride compared to some others.

1515 SW Fifth Avenue

Located within an atrium, this ride takes you up nine floors in a very elegant fashion. The atrium is a pleasant place to spend a quiet moment on a rainy day. Rated the best in-door glass elevator.

U.S. National Bank
Fifth and Burnside

There are three sets of elevators: floors 1-17; 18-30; and the expresses—smooth but fast from 1-30 and 30-43. It travels a swooshing 30-feet-per-second. A restaurant comfortable for kids is being built on the 27th floor. This elevator ride is rated the longest.

Portland City Parking Garage
Between Fourth and Fifth, and Alder and Washington $

This is one to press your nose against to get the full effect. For just 60 cents you can spend an hour going up and down on one of the city's best outside glass elevator rides. If you enter on the blue track you can ride from the 10th floor down. If you enter on the orange track you'll get nine floors of pure thrill. It's exciting! And it's open 24-hours-a-day, except Sunday.

This is also the place to ride down one of the city's curviest enclosed streets. Park up on the top level, outside, and when you leave you'll wind around and around and around and around until you reach the pay booth. A sure way to make all passengers ill, dizzy or thrilled.

First Interstate Bank
1300 SW Fifth

Rated the fastest and the sickest! (See **METRO TRIVIA**)

Pioneer Court House
Fifth, between Yamhill and Morrison

Rated the fanciest.

BUS

Tri-Met Services $

For some interesting bus rides which will give you wonderful views of the city and Metro neighborhoods, try these:

No. 77 Beltline, 231-3177

Tri-Met's longest bus ride. You'll travel through Washington County, Portland Transit Mall, into northeast Portland and back downtown and out into SW Portland and Lake Oswego. You will see many different views of Portland and the Metro area. A guaranteed two hour's worth!

No. 5 Interstate, 231-3105

This ride will take you from Vancouver, Washington to Portland Transit Mall and out to Sherwood. You'll cross three rivers and travel in two states!

No. 31 Estacada, 231-3231

Goes from Portland Transit Mall to Estacada the long way. See numerous farms dotting the countryside.

No. 18 Troutdale, 231-3118

A great way to see Portland's east side and the east Metro area. Travel from Portland Transit Mall out to Gresham and surrounding area.

No. 63 Washington Park Zoo, 231-3263

Ride the famous bus, painted by Portland artist Scott McIntire. Leaves from Fifth and SW Washington downtown Portland every hour.

For more information on bus trips contact:
Call A Bus System — 231-3199
Call for Current Fares — 233-3511
Handicap Information — 231-4952

Most trips turn around at the end of the line and return by the same route. Try creating you own special return trip.

HELICOPTER

Hillsboro Helicopter $
1040 NE 25th, 648-2831

It's the home of "Skyview Traffic Watch". On Saturday you can get a helicopter ride for $10, for those two years of age and over.

AIRPLANE

AAR Western Skyways $
Troutdale Airport, 665-1181

You can get a discount (usually under $10), on a plane ride if you are with a small group.
Directions: Exit No. 17 east off I-84, east of Portland.

BOATS

Canby Ferry Crossing: Molalla River State Park

You'll travel through the country, with large farms on either side of the highway. The ferry trip takes about five minutes from shore to shore with four cars per ride.

For an added outing, head up the road from the ferry on Locust Street, to 37th Avenue, and look for signs to Molalla River State Park. Here at the park three rivers meet—the Pudding, Willamette and Molalla.

There are complete park/picnic facilities, including a boat launch. There's also a foot bridge through a very marshy area where you'll find lots of live kermits.
Directions: Take I-205 to Stafford exit. Head south on Stafford Road to Mountain Road, to the Willamette River. Ferry crossings run daily from 10 am to 7 pm. Free.

Columbia Gorge Sternwheeler
P.O. Box 307
Cascade Locks, 374-8290 $

Ride on a replica of a turn of the century sternwheeler. Full food and beverage service is available. The trip usually takes about two hours and travels on the Columbia River up and down the Gorge. Sometimes the Sternwheeler is moored in Portland, but it is usually moored at Cascade Locks Marine Park.

Directions: Take exit No. 44 off I-84 East. Amtrak stops at Cascade Locks if you want to leave the car at home and combine boat and train ride. Call Amtrak for schedule.

TRAINS

Northwest Live Steamers
Molalla
Noon until 5 pm, open every nice Sunday during the summer.

These are small trains pulled by real steam engines. You can ride on the small cars around a park-like setting. Bring a lunch and have a picnic. Two times a year, usually in July, this is the home of the Steam Up celebration which brings train buffs from all over.

Directions: South on I-5 from Portland, take the Woodburn exit, head for Molalla. Go through Molalla. Just past the city limits the road come to a T. Turn right. Next you will encounter two Y's; stay to your left each time. The second Y has a sign advertising Northwest Live Steamers. Approximately 2.2 miles from center of Molalla.

Washington Park Zoo Train $

Both an open and a covered railroad train operate at the Washington Park Zoo during normal Zoo hours. During the winter months, the trains operate only on weekends, weather permitting. You can board at the Zoo and get off at the Rose Test Gardens—reboard later and return to the Zoo. Or you can begin your trip at the Rose Gardens.

You will see behind-the-scene activities of the Zoo and enjoy lots of forest and park surroundings.

Chelatchie Prairie Train
Battle Ground, Wash.
Call for schedules, 206-687-7428

Although the pace is a mere 10 mph, excitement mounts as this train travels over track laid in 1898. Riders pass through a 300-foot-long tunnel and cross the Lewis River on an 85-foot-high trestle.

On arriving at Moulton Falls Park, there is the option of catching a later train back to the depot, or limiting the stopover to a quick 20 minutes while the engine is switched. The park is picnic-perfect.

Directions: From I-5 or I-205 take Battle Ground exit and follow signs to downtown Battle Ground (approximately 10 miles). Depot is on Main Street at railroad crossing.

Amtrak
Portland, 248-1146   ($)

For a short, delightful train ride, board either at the Union Station in Portland, at 800 NW Sixth Ave., and ride across the Columbia River to Vancouver, to the train depot at Burlington Northern Station at the end of West 11th Avenue: or reverse the trip. The trip is less than 30 minutes, but you will get the feel of travel by rail. Call for reservations. For a longer outing, take Amtrak to Hood River and back.

TAXI   ($)

Take a short trip through downtown or your neighborhood. It gets expensive, but how many children have had the opportunity to ride a taxi in Portland? When did you take your last taxi ride?

Bring a bit of New York to the West Coast

Broadway Cab — 227-1234
New Rose City Cab — 282-7707
Portland Taxi — 256-5400
Radio Cab — 227-1212

BIKES

Tom McCall Waterfront Park to South Waterfront

A paved pathway runs along the Willamette River seawall, south from the Steel Bridge, to the South Waterfront Project, located just south of the Hawthorne Bridge. The river is on one side and the city on the other. You will travel under three city bridges; see the steel sculpture by Bruce West near the Burnside Bridge, where many summer concerts are enjoyed.

Across the street you can visit the Saturday Market from April-December. Just south, along the seawall, you'll find the Oregon Battleship Memorial. There is limited access to the river's edge by the seawall. Best access is in the South Waterfront area.

Tryon Creek State Park
11321 SW Terwilliger

Three miles of paved off-road bike paths within the park. The paths are gently sloped. You'll ride among tall firs and small creatures. Nice and cool on a hot sunny day and fairly protected from the rain. For a more challenging ride there is a way to connect with Terwilliger bike path ending 8 miles later at Duniway Park.

Kruse Way
Lakegrove

Take I-5 south to 217 exit. Take 217 toward Lake Oswego, Kruse Way. Bike path is on your left. Across from Mercantile Village turn left on Daniel Way. Park near Safeco Insurance, a large white building on north side. Begin ride in front of Safeco. Head east along Kruse Way. Path ends just east of I-5. Turn around and return to Mercantile Village for a cool drink. The path is off the street and very flat—good for beginning young cyclist. Under 2 miles in length.

On one side there is busy highway traffic, on the other it's farm land with cows. But hurry—a shopping center will be going in someday.

Willamette Park to John's Landing

Park at Willamette Park. There is a charge during the summer months and it's very crowded on weekends. Start your bike trip on the paved pathway which runs throughout the park. Head north towards the city center. The paved trail ends but keep going onto the gravel/dirt road. Willamette Sailing Club is on your right and railroad tracks on your left. Look for a bike symbol, "Willamette Greenway Trail". This is private property but you are permitted to cycle or walk through during daylight. The pathway is paved and travels next to the river's edge. There are places to stop and get down to the river; rocks and sand to sit by. Trail ends at Boundary Street, across from John's Landing.

SE 28th to Westmoreland Park

Look for bike signs north of SE Steele on 28th, just before the Rhododendron Test Gardens. This is a very short but scenic off-street paved pathway. You will ride past the Rhododendron Gardens which is an interesting place to visit in all seasons. From there the path goes along the Eastmoreland Public Golf Course and onto Bybee Street. This will take you up and over McLoughlin Boulevard. Here you may cross Bybee to enjoy the many activities in Westmoreland Park. You return on the same route.

Note: This neighborhood is a good place for young riders. The sidewalks are smooth and wide and blocks are very long.

Mt. Tabor Park

The reservoirs above 60th Avenue provide a long unbroken sidewalk for beginning cyclists. It is also a great place to skate or to push dollies' new carriage.

George Rogers Park (See **PARKS**)

Greenway Park (See **PARKS**)

SHOPS

Let's face it, we are a culture dependent on large shopping centers and huge chain stores. Our kids think that all food comes pleasantly wrapped in colorful packages, and they seldom experience anything but the impersonal efficiency of these cavernous rotundas of consumerism. We have included a sampling of Portland's most interesting smaller stores to encourage you to rediscover, with your children, the fun and surprises that these places offer.

Remember these small stores are all in business, so try to go at off hours when shopping is not so hectic, and in very small groups. It would seem a good idea, also, to notify the proprietor, when possible, of an impending visit of a group.

Buy something if you can, particularly if you spend a great deal of time in the store. For grocery stores it might be fun to plan a meal ahead of time. Or just pick out interesting looking foods to take home to sample.

When visiting ethnic grocery stores, prepare the children ahead of time for cultural differences in choices of foods. This is a good opportunity to teach that which is strange to one culture may be a delicacy somewhere else. Many of the small grocery stores are family operated, and frequently serve as community centers for a particular ethnic group. Often the clerks speak little or no English and you'll have to get by on lots of smiles. This can be a fun or frightening experience for a child, depending on how you handle it.

SPECIALITY STORES

Comella and Son and Daughter Fruits and Vegetables
6956 SW Garden Home Rd., 245-5033

The southwest's version of Corno's, and then some. Frank Comella comes by to greet you with a warm smile and always a sample of delicious fruit or vegetable. A wonderful deli, beautiful flowers and plants are available.

Nature's
3437 NE 24th, 388-3414

A health food store gone gourmet! Nature's is the largest store in the Portland area devoted to natural products and remedies. Here you will find incredibly artistic arangements of chemical-free fruits and vegetables. There are fresh and dried pastas of every shape, size and kind. You can even grind your own peanut butter. Food items are in bulk and more traditional packaging. Nature's also carries non-food items such as kitchen wares, natural shampoos, body lotions and soaps. It is a place that proves shopping can be fun!

Corno's
711 SE Union, 232-3157

You can't miss Corno's. It's the place with the big cornucopia of brightly painted fruit all around the outside of the building. It looks like Carmen Miranada's headgear. As a major supplier to area restaurants and grocers, Corno's begins business each day before most people wake up. In addition to a large selection of fresh produce, Corno's carries a wide assortment of bulk items: from nuts to pasta to dried fruits. You can get almost anything in enormous institutional size cans or jars. Kids might also enjoy going around in back to see them unload the big trucks of produce.

Troy's Seafood Markets
11130 SE Powell, 760-2566
3050 SW Cedar Hills Blvd., 646-4184
816 NE Grand, 231-1477
15900 SW Boones Ferry Rd., 635-6201

Tanks with live lobster, crabs, clams, oysters, mussels and even eels.

Ocean King Seafood
Corner of Fourth and NW Davis, 222-0092

Ocean King is an oriental seafood and meat market. You can find almost anything here from live crabs and frogs to geese feet and pork bellies. There are fresh fish, squid and octopus, as well as more exotic frozen fish.

New Shin Shin Market
2001 SE Stark, 232-9911

This market is Korean. In addition to the usual oriental foods and special Korean products, it also has a Korean video lending library and many Korean books, magazines and tapes for sale.

Anzen Importers
736 NE Union, 233-5111

Japanese foods and import goods: watch the butcher prepare fresh sashmi.

Dong Phuong Market
839 N Killingsworth, 283-3957

Indochinese. This small store carries everything from yard goods to videotapes. Notice the exquisite packaging on the cosmetics and medicines.

Asia Market and Restaurant
5325 E Burnside, 232-4454

Busy, friendly, market that sells groceries as well as Indochinese toys and magazines. A restaurant is included in the market.

Vieng Lao
1032 N Killingsworth, 285-7833

When we visited this market it was crowded with families and children. Like most of these small markets, it carries an assortment of toys and household items not common in the local chain store.

Fong Chong
301 NW Fourth Ave., 223-1777

A good place to explore Chinese food products. The store has a large selection of foods from all over the Orient. There is also dim sum carry-out and a dim sum restaurant next door.

Beccerra Elda
108 NE 28th St., 234-7785

This Spanish market carries mostly canned goods. There is also a small selection of Spanish magazines, greeting cards and candies.

Le Panier
71 SW Second St., 241-3524
Clackamas Town Center, 659-5587
Yamhill Market, 110 SW Yamhill, 241-5613

French bakery. The SW Second location is the largest store. There is a tremendous assortment of breads in amazing shapes and sizes. And delicious pastries are baked all day long. Huge ovens are out front so kids can watch the loaves of bread baked. The smells are wonderful. Impossible to leave without something in your mouth.

John's Import Autowrecking
733 NW Everett, 222-1601

This is a seven story department-store-style wrecking yard located right in downtown Portland. Wrecked cars are organiz-ed by make: i.e. Volvo & Porsches on one floor. Datsuns &

Toyotas on another. People looking for specific parts buy them directly off a wrecked car. The floors are shiny and clean. **Note:** Scheduled sightseeing 10-12 weekdays. Tours available. Call in advance.

Boyd's Pet Shop
5540 E Burnside, 232-6830

Boyd's is one of the oldest and most pleasant pet stores in town. They carry all kinds of small animals: kittens, fish, birds, mice and rabbits. (Must go elsewhere for reptiles.)

Pet N' Pond
14405 SW Pacific Hwy.
Tigard, Canterbury Square, 620-1226

Well known for their great selection of exotic birds, fish and reptiles. Includes many items for caring for small pets.

Strictly R/C
7868 SW Capital Hwy., 244-3356

Everything you need for radio control model airplane flying. Lots of colorful models hanging from ceiling.

Aero Sports
2509 SE 119th St., 761-1611
2700 NW 185th St., Tanasbourne Town Center, 645-8923

These stores sell all-around hobby accessories for ships, trains and cars.

Bob's Whistle Stop
14037 SE Stark, 252-7118

Specializing in model trains. Carries all gauges and models for the budding as well as the established train buff.

Vic's Hobby Shop
1725 NE 40th St., 281-1032

You'll find not only a variety of model trains and accessories, but the store is noted for carrying "Billing Ship Models" which are large, intricate, masted ships.

Holland Feed and Garden Supply
12250 SW Broadway
Beaverton, 644-3400

You will find yourself in the midst of bales of hay, sacks of grain, and other animal feed at the Holland Feed store. This store serves as a food and equipment supplier for farm animals large and small. You can learn what to feed a baby pig, or buy a harness for your pet pony. There is also a small pet store and garden shop.

Hollywood Portland Costumes
3121 NE Sandy, 235-9215

Take a giant step into the world of make-believe. This is a great place for kids to explore the looks of past and future. You can create the most awesome costumes, be anything or anyone you want to be. The store has racks of costumes and accessories, masks and makeup.

Oregon Wholesale Novelties
902 SW Yamhill, 226-3841

The last of the great stores where a kid can find something for a nickle. You can buy music makers, hats, masks, horns, party favors, dress-up items and surprises!
Note: Adult book and card section.

Callin Novelties—Magician Supplies
412 SW Fourth St., 223-4821

In addition to carrying everything an aspiring magician could desire, Callin Novelties carries games, novelties and party items. Best of all, between 12-5:30 Monday through Friday, and 12-4:30 pm Saturday, there is a magician in the store to

demonstrate tricks and help you pick out items.
Note: A small, Adult's Only section.

Apple Music
225 SW First Ave., 226-0036

Whether you are putting together a rock band or discovering the joys of sound, a visit to Apple Music is a must. Guitars in every shape, size and color line the walls. Gigantic sound systems are stacked to the ceiling. Drums, cymbals and keyboards are at your fingertips. This is a store that allows reasonable "hands-on" experience, and you don't need to worry about noise.

Miniature House
521 SW 10th St., 227-4997

Create a dream house. Miniature House contains almost everything you could imagine—in miniature. It ranges from the extravagant to the affordable. See Victorian doll houses filled with people and furniture. You can even buy a small cat to sit by your small hearth.

The Military Corner
2729 NE Sandy, 287-6088

Almost every game of strategy imaginable as well as books on games, can be found at the Military Corner. The store also carries military models and miniatures, metal figures, and the paints and supplies to go with them.

Portland Sports Card Company
1814 NE 33rd, 284-7126

Haul out your old baseball card collection, and if you don't have one, here is the place to start. There are expensive collector's cards (the ones your mother threw away when you

were twelve), current cards, card albums, sports magazines, and even comic books.

Hippo Hardware and Trading Company
201 SE 12th Ave., 231-1444

A second-hand store with "hands-on" philosophy. There are four floors of old and new tools and antiques of many varieties. School tours available.

Red Spirit Creations
214 NW Couch, 223-6220

This is a non-profit store operated by the Urban Indian Council. Here you'll find unique and beautiful creations hand-crafted by local Indian community members. Classes are offered in the art of beading, the making of moccasins and coin purses, and the construction of rawhide drums.

Windplay
232 SW Ankeny, 223-1760

This store is easy to spot—it's the one with the colorful kites flying high out front. Inside look up to see kites hanging from the ceiling in all sorts of colors and shapes. Kits, materials and classes are available. All you need after a visit to this store is a great wind!

Paul Schuback—Violin Shop
3003 SE Milwaukie, 239-4430

Will schedule tours to see the making of a violin. Shop violins have won awards worldwide.

SHOPPING CENTERS

As parents of young children know, a shopping center is one place to head in bad weather. This is particularly true when you go at off hours to avoid crowds and kids have a bit more freedom to exorcise those rainy day demons.

All shopping centers are good places for window shopping and people watching. Most have some type of fountain or interesting sculptures. We list a few of the local shopping centers that offer special features of interest to kids.

Jantzen Beach Center
I-5, Jantzen Beach Exit

Antique Carousel (see **RIDES**); video arcade with machines for even the toddler; hydrotube; pet store; movie theater. (see **WALKS** for additional ideas.)

Clackamas Town Center
1200 SE 82nd St.

Ice Capades Chalet—ice skating (see **SPORTS**); restaurants overlooking ice rink; pet store.
Note: The elevators are hard to find and it is difficult to get from one level to another with strollers and wheelchairs.

Lloyd Center
Between NE Weidler and Multnomah

Lloyd Center Ice Pavilion—ice skating. (see **SPORTS**)

Eastport Plaza
4000 SE 82nd St.
Highway 217, Washington Square exits

Hydrotube. (see **SPORTS**)

Washington Town Square

Hydrotube (see **SPORTS**); restaurant overlooking the hydrotube.

Galleria
921 SW Morrison

Sky bridges to parking lot; high, brightly lit open space in center of building; long escalator ride between floors.

Saturday Market
Below the Burnside Bridge off Front Avenue
Portland
Hours: Weekends, April through December, 9-5 pm.

It is uncertain whether more people go to Saturday Market to eat or to shop. Both can be an almost overwhelming experience. Going into its 10th year, Saturday Market has maintained its tradition of featuring quality crafts and delicious food at reasonable prices. The same craftspeople are not there every weekend and there are frequently mimes or musicians performing so every visit can be a unique experience.

Yamhill Market
110 SW Yamhill

Here you'll discover small shops and stands. There is also a glass-enclosed elevator with a view of the center of the building—slow, gentle ride good for young kids. Food bars serving a variety of international delights; attractive produce and seafood markets; bakery, chocolate and nut shops.

New Market Theatre
213 SW Ash

This newly restored building was originally designed as a market with a theater on the upper floor. Efforts are continuing to bring small shops and restaurants back into the building. (See **EXCURSIONS**)

SHOPPING FOR KIDS

TOY STORES

Child's Play
715 NW 23rd, 224-5586

A wonderful assortment of toys from all over the world. There is a play area for tots while you browse. Get on the mailing list for their very informative newsletter.

Finnegan's Toys and Gifts
922 SW Yamhill, 221-0306

Almost as much fun for adults as for children. A spectacular selection of wind-up toys in the back of the store, along with a platform on which you can watch them run amok. The store is also great for sticker-collectors.

City Kids
810 SW Second, 224-5784

Fantasy land for children and adults. High quality toys and gifts with a European flair. A second store is planned for Washington Square.

Mrs. Tiggly Winkles
Water Tower, John's Land, 227-7084

The usual and unusual in handcrafted original clothing and toys for children. A small selection of well-made wooden playthings for the under-five set.

Mrs. Twichets Toy Shoppe
425 Second St., Lake Oswego, 635-8697

Unique European educational toys.

The Toy Bear
121 N Main, Gresham, 661-5310

Lots of bears, big and small; dolls; books; and unique gifts.

Toys R' Us
1800 Jantzen Beach Center, 289-4691
12535 SE 82nd St., Milwaukie, 659-5163

Large, overwhelming discount store. Helps to know what you are looking for before entering. Acres of toys and games for all ages — toddlers to adults. Also discount baby needs.

Learning World
720 NE 181st. St., 667-3403
Beaverton Mall, 643-6538
Vancouver Mall, 206-892-8907
Lloyd Center, 287-5731

High quality toys and educational materials.

CHILDREN'S BOOK STORES

Powell Books
1005 W Burnside, 228-4651

New & used books. HUGE store with large children's section. Open long hours and weekends.

Children's Place
1631 NE Broadway, 284-8294

A large assortment of children's records, as well as books. Children can sit in an old-fashioned bathtub to read while parents browse.

Early Childhood Bookhouse
724 NW 23rd., 224-6372

Parenting and teaching resources. Books for beginning readers.

Skidmore Village Children's Books
50 SW Third, 222-5076

Carries a large selection of hard cover and paperbacks, and also delightful cards and gifts.

Ginger & Pickles Bookstore for Children
425 Second St., Lake Oswego, 636-5438

A large selection of foreign titles, as well as standard classics. The shop has a laminating machine.

Annie Bloom's
7829 SW Capital Hwy., 246-0053

A large variety of both hard and soft cover books, with a cozy area just for kids.

CLOTHING RESALE

Second Generation
3959 SE Hawthorne Blvd., 233-8130

Dressame Street
2812 SE Courtney Rd., Milwaukie, 653-5448

Gingerbread Express
4410 NE Tillamook, 284-2908

Small Fry
2428 NE Broadway, 284-9705

Wee Three
4825 SW Hall Rd., Beaverton, 644-5953

METRO TRIVIA

Metro Trivia is miscellaneous bits and pieces of information to titilate the imagination and curiousity of young and old. We offer the following, sometimes unsubstantiated, trivia in the spirit of fun and challenge.

We welcome any additions or corrections you might wish to make to Metro Trivia. Please write us at Discovery Press, P.O. 12241, Portland, Oregon 97212.

• Back in 1845, Francis Pettygrove and Asa Lovejoy tossed an 1835 penny to decide what to name our city. Pettygrove won two out of the three tosses, naming our city after his home town, Portland, Maine. The loser was Boston.

• Portland can boast having both the largest and smallest park in the United States. The largest is Forest Park with over 4,700 acres, and the smallest is Mills End Park at Front Avenue and Yamhill. Portland's narrowest park is McCarthy Park at Swan Island.

• Towers, tunnels and tires: The park with the most playground structures: Greenway Park, Beaverton.

• The tallest building is the First Interstate Bank at 1300 SW Fifth Ave. It reaches 546 feet from the sidewalk up. The U.S. National Bank at SW Fifth and Burnside, is second at 436 feet 10 inches.

• The fastest ride in the west (elevator ride) is located in the First Interstate Bank, 1300 SW Fifth. A sure way to make you turn green in seconds.

• Best outside elevator ride is found at the City Center Parking Garage, SW Fourth and Morrison. Be sure to press your nose against the window to receive the full effect.

• Portland can boast about its streets, too! To drive the curviest street, start at the intersection of SW Dosch, Patton, Humphrey and Talbot Roads. Take Talbot to Fairmont Boulevard (keep to your left at the intersections). Stay on Fairmont, making a circle back to the intersection where you started. This time continue on to Humphrey Boulevard to the Scholls Ferry Road intersection. From there take Hewitt Boulevard back to Patton and you'll end up once again at the intersection. You've just completed a gigantic figure eight! If you're not carsick by now there must be something wrong, so do it again!

• For the curviest drive in an enclosed area try the City Center Parking Garage, SW Fourth and Alder entrance (blue track side). Park up on top and when you leave you'll wind around and around in a corkscrew pattern until you reach the exit.

• The longest street in Portland is believed to be Burnside: It's over 20 miles. It runs from east county, through northeast, across the river and into southwest.

• The shortest street is SW Isabella off Vista—only 80 feet in length!

• The steepest street is SW College. Follow Hall Street to Upper Hall, to 16th Avenue. At College Street, turn east and head down to 12th Avenue. Be sure your brakes are working!

• The first paved street in Portland was at NW 26th Avenue and Thurman, and served as the entrance to the Lewis and Clark Exposition in 1905.

• The busiest streets in Portland are McLoughlin Boulevard with 46,000 trips per day; and Powell Boulevard with over 35,000 trips per day.

• The best sled ride in town, of course, is located near the steepest street. Begin at SW 16th, up near Elizabeth Street. Continue down 16th, turning right onto Upper Hall Street, and ending around 14th Avenue, near Portland State University. Most all of the cross streets dead-end. The traffic is light and slow except for you!

• The first Portland bridge over the Willamette River was the Morrison Bridge. The original one was built in 1887, out of wood. The Morrison Bridge is also the busiest bridge in the city.

• The Steel Bridge is the only bridge in the world that has a double-decker lift. The railroad bridge can be lifted independently from the car bridge. It's known as the largest elevator in the world.

• Portland has two castles! One is made out of large stones, and has a drawbridge and moat. It is on SW Fairview, near Bennington. The other is on SW Buckingham Street and is made of bricks. See if you can find them. One you can see from the 405 Freeway, near the SW Sixth Avenue exit.

• The most colorful house in the metro area is located at 805 W 15th Street, Vancouver. The owners have painted each brick, stone and board a different color. The backyard is a visual potpourri. Every inch is covered with small plastic miniatures as well as appropriate plastic environments for each. The gates say "Welcome" and children are just that.

• Northwest Portland has the densest population between San Francisco and Seattle.

• The first land claim in Portland was by William Johnson in 1842. He built a log cabin at what is now SW Curry and Macadam Street. A historical marker designates the almost inaccessible site. It is near SW Curry and Macadam, below the I-5 Freeway.

• Perhaps the most daring of all stunts was done by Silas Christofferson when he became the first pilot ever to take-off from the top of a building, the Multnomah Hotel, now known as the Multnomah, 319 SW Pine, in 1912. Both pilot and plane survived.

• The largest lake in the metropolitan area is Vancouver Lake located in the state of Washington.

• The highest spot in Portland is on top of Council Crest: elevation 1,074 feet above sea level.

• The lowest spot in Portland is the Delta Park area which is around 10 feet above sea level.

• The first framed house was put up by Captain Nathaniel Crosby, great-grandfather of the late Bing Crosby. This structure, built in 1847 at SW Front and Washington, is no longer standing.

• The oldest home still standing is the Stephens Home, built for James Stephens, who founded East Portland. The home, which is located at SE 12th Avenue and Stephens Street, was built in 1864. It no longer has its fine cupola and holds little of its past splendor.

• Another old home, built in 1872-3, is the Kamm Home built for Joseph Kamm. Located at 1425 SW 20th Ave., it is in the process of being restored to its original beauty.

• The first public building in Portland was a jail erected in 1851, by Colonel William King, near First and Oak. But the oldest municipal building is the Pioneer Courthouse, still standing at Sixth and Morrison, built in 1875.

• The first school built from public taxes was at the present site of Pioneer Square at SW Fifth and Morrison. The school was dedicated on May 17, 1858.

• The oldest apple tree in the Northwest is off I-5 and Highway 14, Vancouver. Once surrounded by freeway, the tree now has a small park of its own. To reach it, walk through a refurbish-

ed railroad underpass along Columbia Way. When a young sailor left his sweetheart in England, she gave him apple seeds from the dessert served at his farewell party. The young woman asked the sailor to plant the seeds when he reached the Northwest Territory. Legend has it that he did just that in 1826.

• In 1851 John Preston, the first Surveyor General of Oregon, placed "the starting stake" for all land surveys to be conducted in the Pacific Northwest. The stake, replaced by stone, is called the Willamette Stone. You'll find the historical marker off SW Skyline Boulevard just north of Burnside Street.

• Frank Beach is the man who nicknamed our city the "Rose City".

• Portland is the carousel capital of the United States.

CALENDAR

The Calendar is a month by month listing of events of special interest to kids which occur each year at roughly the same time. The list is intended to alert you to watch the media or call for more up-to-date information on these events. Since there will likely be scheduling variations from year to year, we suggest that you check the Calendar a month or so ahead.

Good places to look for the specifics on these events and other current activities for children are:

Portland Family Calendar
Oregonian, Friday's "Serendipity Section"
Willamette Week, "Fresh Weekly"
Downtowner

There are many places such as OMSI that have continuously changing exhibits and will gladly provide you with their own schedules. (See **RESOURCES** section of this book.)
Abbreviations:
CC — Community College
WFC — Western Forestry Center by Washington Park Zoo, 4033 SW Canyon Road.
MC — Memorial Coliseum, 1401 N Wheeler
MCEC — Multnomah County Expo Center, 2060 N Marine Drive
PSU — Portland State University, 724 SW Harrison
PIR — Portland International Raceway, West Delta Park

January

World's Toughest Rodeo — MC
Oregon Dog Show — MCEC
All Breed Dog Show - MCEC
Northwest Agriculture Show — MCEC
Auto Show — MC

February

Cat Fancier's Show — MC
Sportsman's Show — MCEC
Walt Disney's Magic Kingdom On Ice — MC
Portland Boat Show — MCEC
Furniture Makers' Show — WFC
Ice Follies — MC
Agate and Mineral Rock Show — OMSI
Lewis & Clark International Fair — Lewis & Clark College

March

Northwest Food Fair — MC
Barbershop Ballad Contest — Forest Grove
Gay '90s Festival — Forest Grove
Roadster Show — MC
Oregon Archeological Society Show — OMSI
International Gem & Mineral Show — MC
St. Patrick's Day Parade — SW Broadway, Burnside to Main
Go-Kart Races — PIR
Northwest Quilt Show — PSU, Smith Center Ballroom
Meier & Frank "Countryside Farm" — Meier & Frank, downtown store
Shrine Circus — MC

April

Trillium Festival — Tryon Creek State Park
Saturday Market Opening — Under the Burnside Bridge
Arbor Day — Plant A Tree! — Check local parks
Portland Antique Car Club Swap Meet — MC
Home and Garden Show — MCEC
Farm Animals & Easter Bunnies — Lloyd Center
Hawaiian Festival — Forest Grove, Pacific University
Breakfast with the Easter Bunny — Frederick & Nelson, downtown store
Peter Rabbit Easter Breakfast — Meier & Frank, downtown store

Easter Egg Hunt — Alpenrose Dairy
Toy & Doll Show — MC
Bird Sculptures in Wood Show — WFC
Lego Road Show — Washington Square

May

Earth Week — Activities at many locations
World's Greatest Tricycle Race — Mt. Hood CC
Old Time Fiddlers' Contest — Clackamas CC
Go-Kart Races — PIR
St. Johns Parade Days — Cathedral Park
Truck Show — MCEC
GI Joe Fish-In — Westmoreland Park
Children's Day — Japanese Gardens
Renaissance Faire — Lewis & Clark College

June

Rose Festival Portland — A city-wide celebration
    Starlight Parade
    Jr. Rose Festival Parade
    Festival of Bands
    Grande Floral Parade
    Rose Festival Fun Center
    Ship Tours
    Little Britches Rodeo
Timber Festival — Molalla
Strawberry Festival — Wilsonville
Sesame Street Live — MC
Your Zoo and All That Jazz — Wednesday evening Jazz
Concerts at Zoo
Zoograss Bluegrass Concert — Thursday evenings at Zoo
Cascade Runoff — downtown Portland
Hillsboro Happy Days — Hillsboro
Gymanfa Ganu Festival- (Welsh) — Bryn Seion Church,
Beavercreek
Ft. Vancouver Days — Vancouver

July

Molalla Buckaroo
Little Buckaroo Rodeo — Mt. Hood CC
Pro Ski Races — Timberline Lodge
Annual Torchlight Skidown — Timberline Lodge
All Breed Dog Show — MCEC
Fireworks:
  Portland Civic Stadium
  Oaks Park
  Ft. Vancouver — Vancouver
  Timber Park — Estacada
  Lake Oswego
  Happy Valley Park
  Washington Co. Fairgrounds — Hillsboro
Scottish Highland Games and Clan Gathering — David
Douglas High School
Neighborfair — Tom McCall Waterfront Park
Bluegrass Festival — Hillsboro
Robin Hood Festival — Sherwood City Park
Summer Moonlight Festival — Rose Garden Amphitheater,
Washington Park
Woodturning Show — WFC
Concours d'elegance — Forest Grove
  (Vintage, antique and classic autos)
Estacada Timber Festival — Estacada
Multnomah County Fair
Wooden Boat Show — WFC
Chamber Music Northwest
Outdoor concerts in city parks — Portland Park Bureau

August

Washington County Fair
Clark County Fair
Clackamas County Fair
Elephant Roundup/Asian Culture Festival — Zoo

Tigard Town & Country Days — Cook Park, Tigard
Tualatin Crawfish Festival — Tualatin
Mt. Hood Jazz Festival — Mt. Hood CC
Bluegrass On The Mountain Concert — Timber Park,
Estacada
Pickle Family Circus
Annual Air Show — Evergreen Airport, Vancouver
Classic Music Concert — Washington Park
Oregon State Fair

September

International Timber Festival — Estacada Timber Park,
Estacada
Best of the Northwest Tug Boat Races — Oregon City
Lipizzan Stallion Show — MC
Log Home and Early American Crafts — WFC
Autumnfest — Old Town, Portland
Artquake — South Park Blocks, Portland
Oktoberfest — Holladay Park, Lloyd Center, Portland
Mt. Angel Oktoberfest — Mt. Angel
Vancouver Sausage Festival — St. Joseph's School,
Vancouver
Ringling Brothers Circus — Show and animals, walk from
NW Hoyt and 10th across Broadway Bridge to Coliseum.

Catlin Gabel Rummage Sale — MC
Wintering In Festival — Bybee Howell House

October

Annual Greek Holiday Festival — Holy Trinity Greek Or-
thodox Church
Portland Regional Gem & Mineral Show — MCEC
Bonsai Show — WFC/Japanese Gardens
Portland Miniature Show — MC
Handmade Furniture Show — WFC
Portland International Livestock Exposition — MCEC

Raffi in Concert — Children's Place Bookstore
Spook Train — Zoo
Haunted Houses — Portland J.C.'s

November

Verboort Kraut and Sausage Festival — Verboort
Baby and Family Fair — MC
"Nutcracker" — Ballet West
Festival of Trees — MC
Wooden Toy Display — WFC
Ice Capades — MC
Model Train Association, open to the public — 283-TRAIN

December

Breakfast with Santa — Meier & Frank
Cinnamon Bear — Frederick and Nelson
Talking Tree — downtown Meier & Frank
Rudolph — Mall 205
Peacock Lane — 39th Street, Portland (lights)
Storybook Lane Christmas — Alpenrose Dairy
Christmas Lights Parade of Ships on Columbia/Willamette
River
Sing Your Own Messiah — Auditiorium
Messiah — Civic Auditorium
International Christmas Tree Show — WFC
Holiday Woodcarving Show — WFC
Ethnic Christmas Display — WFC
"Nutcracker" — Jr. Civic Theater
Doll House and Miniature Show — MCEC
Toy & Doll Show — MCEC
All-Breed Cat Show — MCEC
Cut your own Christmas Tree — Portland Visitor's Center
for locations
All-Breed Bench Dog Show — MC
Teddy Bear Clinic — Emanuel Hospital

RESOURCES

We have included a list of some materials to help you continue your explorations of Portland.

BROCHURES AND MAPS

- "Discover the Wild Side of Portland", a list of all major Portland parks with maps and a chart indicating facilities and equipment. It includes suggestions for activities like walking, fishing, etc. Available at Portland's Visitor's Center, Portland Parks Bureau.

- "Forest Park", easy to read map and access to Forest Park information. Available at Portland Visitor's Center, Portland Parks Bureau.

- "Getting There by Bike", bicycle map for the Portland metropolitan area. Available in some book stores, Metropolitan Service District, 527 SW Hall Street.

PERIODICALS

- Portland Family Calendar
  1819 NW Everett, 220-0459

    A monthly guide to what is going on of interest to children and families in the Portland area. Also feature articles and regular columns.

- **Oregonian**
  1320 SW Broadway, 221-8240

    Daily newspaper. Friday's "Serendipity" section contains listings of special events.

- **Willamette Week
Downtowner**

Free weekly publication with sections listing special events. Distributed on street corners and in neighborhood stores.

BOOKS

- **Portland Walkbook**

By Peggy Robinson, 1978. An excellent resource for walks/hikes. Usable directions and descriptions. Available in most bookstores.

- **Portland Names and Neighborhoods: Their Historic Origins**

Early Portland: Stump-Town Triumphant

By Eugene E. Snyder. Interesting information about Portland history. Both books available in bookstores or Multnomah County Library.

- **Circling the City**

Guide to handicapped accessibility of public places in and near Portland. Published by the Junior League. Available at Portland Visitor's Center, Easter Seal Society, Junior League.

- **Portland's Public Art, A Guide and History**

By Norma Catherine Gleason, Chet Orloff. Available at Historical Society and area bookstores.

SOURCES

The following list of organizations are either good sources of information or have activities of specific interest to children and families. Many have their own catalogs as well as having important events listed in other periodicals. If you want a complete list of activities it is best to contact the organizations directly.

- **Portland Visitors and Convention Center**
  26 SW Salmon St., 222-2223

  Across from Willamette Center. Park on river side of Front Avenue in Visitor's Center lot. A first stop in your exploraton of Portland. Great one-stop shopping for maps and brochures. All free or at nominal cost.

- **Vancouver Visitor's Service Division**
  303 E Evergreen, 206-696-8034

  The place to go to find out what is happening in Clark County.

- **Portland Bureau of Parks and Recreation**
  The Portland Building
  1120 SW 5th, Room 502, 796-5193

  Call to get on mailing list for the quarterly guide to hundreds of activities. Community centers and culture centers also have their own brochures on all their numerous programs.

- **Portland Community Schools**

  Classes and activities located in neighborhood schools are sponsored by Portland Park Bureau and Portland Public Schools. Schedules are sent to all Portland residents.

  Portland Park Bureau
  1120 SW Fifth, Rm. 502, 796-5123

  Portland Public Schools
  6318 SW Corbett Street, 244-7543

- **Recreation Services for Disabled Citizens**
  426 NE 12th, 248-4328

Activities, classes and summer camps for special citizens.

• Special Olympics
426 NE 12th, 230-1146

Acitivities for handicapped individuals ages 6 and up. Operates year round.

• Vancouver Parks and Recreation
1009 E McLoughlin Blvd., 206-696-8236

• Outdoor Recreation
426 NE 12th
Portland, 230-4018

Summer outdoor activities. Backpacking, raft trips, day hikes. Call for complete catalog.

• Tualatin Hills Parks and Recreation
15707 SW Walker Rd.
Beaverton, 645-6433

Offers numerous activities and classes for children in the Washington County area. Call to get catalog.

• U.S. Forest Service Headquarters
500 W 12th St.
Vancouver, 206-796-7500

For Mt. St. Helens information.

• Portland Audubon Society
5151 N Cornell Rd., 292-6855

• Multnomah County Library
801 SW 10th Central Branch, 223-7201

Listing of activities available in Central library and neighborhood branches.

- **Children's Museum**
  3037 SW 2nd
  Portland, 248-4587

- **OMSI**
  4015 SW Canyon Rd.
  Portland, 222-2904, 222-2828

- **Washington Park Zoo**
  4002 SW Canyon Rd.
  Portland, 226-1561

- **Walking Tours of Portland**

  John Meynink, 234-4742

  Portland Walking Tours, 223-1017

  Dick Pintarich, 796-5193

INDEX

Photo Credits:

NOTES

NOTES

NOTES

NOTES

NOTES